CORPORATE CHRISTIANITY

CORPORATE CHRISTIANITY

How Double Minded Pastors Are Hi-jacking Christianity

BOBBY E. MILLS

New York

CORPORATE CHRISTIANITY

How Double Minded Pastors Are Hi-jacking Christianity

ISBN 978-1-61448-372-4 paperback
ISBN 978-1-61448-373-1 eBook
Library of Congress Control Number: 2012947598

Morgan James Publishing
The Entrepreneurial Publisher
5 Penn Plaza, 23rd Floor
New York City, New York 10001
(212) 655-5470 office • (516) 908-4496 fax
www.MorganJamesPublishing.com

Cover Design by:
Rachel Lopez
www.r2cdesign.com

Interior Design by:
Bonnie Bushman
bonnie@caboodlegraphics.com

CONTENTS

INTRODUCTION

***Corporate Christianity* is a book** about revolutionary Christianity and radical holiness—that is, the moral integration of *flesh* and *Spirit*. Too often, religion in the twenty-first century is about corporate entertainment and money, and, at the same time, is somewhat formalized and sterile, or nonspiritual. In other words, twenty-first century religion in America is emotional entertainment based on a scheme of religious beliefs that are intellectually sophisticated but doomed to failure because they are based upon worldly half-truths rather than *godly spiritual truths*. Indeed, **"Can the blind lead the blind? Shall they not both fall in the ditch?" (Matt. 6:39)**. *Real Christianity* should not be an escape from our social responsibility to be our *brother's keeper*. In other words, *real Christianity* ought to be an affirmation in action of the *will of God*. The *will of God*, simply put, is that we love God with all of our soul and might, that we love our neighbor as we love ourselves, and that we do unto others as we would have them do to us (Jesus' Great Commandments).

All of the socioeconomic systems of the modern age—capitalism, the free-enterprise system, socialism, communism, and so on—are inherently divisive and so work to make the rich richer and the poor poorer. All socioeconomic systems of the modern age are structured in such a manner so that those who are poor work to make the rich richer. Unfortunately, the poor are the ones who make the rich, rich. Abraham Lincoln said it best: "No man should work and not receive the benefits of his own labor." Human exploitation was not Jesus' intention. True Christianity will bring individuals together; they will have a spirit of collective responsibility, and universal brotherhood under God will emerge: *heaven on earth*.

When the disciples asked Jesus to teach them how to pray, Jesus said, "When you pray, pray in this manner: Our Father, which art in Heaven, hallowed be Thy name. Thy kingdom come. Thy will be done on earth as it is in heaven." When we do the will of God, we have heaven on earth. When we do the will of the devil, we have hell on earth. It's just that simple. To be sure, war is hell, because both the guilty as well as the innocent suffer. Institutional "cultural" racism, then, will not exist if we do the *will of God,* loving one another as God loves us. Racism is a damnable affront to the reality of God. God is ontology (spiritual being), not anthropology. God has no physical (anthropological) likeness.

This book emerged from a need for *spiritually* based information about the interaction between theological concepts and the sociology of the human condition. Unfortunately, as humans we have the tendency to want to live life backwards, because sin does make individuals become their own enemy. The ultimate desire of the devil is to make *self* the enemy, or to make individuals destroy themselves. But since he cannot do it, he must obtain permission from each individual.

In part, the information recorded in this book is based upon personal experience, *some* pastoral experience, and professional college teaching experience. I am a graduate of Colgate Rochester Crozer Divinity School (CRCDS) in Rochester, New York. While studying at CRCDS, I was extremely perplexed concerning the motivation of *some, not all,* of my colleagues pursuing the pastoral ministry. Let me say from the beginning: just like *every individual,* I am a sinner saved by God's grace and *His* divine *gift* of forgiveness. Therefore, this book is not intended to be judgmental, but rather spiritually enlightening. As 1 John 5:11 begins with a record, so shall I.

This is the record of Bobby Eugene Mills; my *spiritual* name given to me by my parents. I was born in my maternal grandparents' home (Hathaway and Bessie Brewton) by a midwife in Spartanburg, South Carolina. Degrees are of this world given to individuals by colleges and universities (Caesar's realm). I earned five from various colleges and universities through hard work and tenacious persistence: an Associate of Arts degree (Friendship College), bachelor's degree in education (Barber-Scotia College), Bachelor's of Divinity in Theology (Colgate Rochester Crozer Divinity School), Master of Arts in Sociology (University of Rochester), and a doctorate in sociology (Syracuse University). I grew up in Hardy Chapel Baptist Church in Spartanburg, South Carolina, and I have held membership in churches in Rochester, New York; Chicago, Illinois; Washington, DC; and metropolitan Houston.

It has been my experience that many pastoral leaders find it extremely difficult to interact with degreed individuals. In fact, many pastoral leaders use the *bully* pulpit to condemn degreed individuals, declaring that there is no place for education in the church, only spirituality. Indeed, it is unfortunate that too many pastoral leaders run the educated out of the church, rather than drawing them to the *cross* of Jesus Christ. Yet **Revelation 1:3** declares, **"Blessed is he that reads, and they that hear the words of this prophecy, and keep those things which are written therein: For the time is at hand."** It is clear to me that if individuals cannot read, they cannot understand the Bible, because the Bible is written in *metaphorical* and *allegorical* terms. For example, Jesus talked about having the faith of a mustard seed. Or that it is as difficult for a rich man to go to heaven as it is for a camel to go through the eye of a needle. Therefore, the ability to read, comprehend, and understand indeed are flip sides of the same coin. Solomon declared, **"Wisdom is good with an inheritance: And by it there is profit to them that see the sun. For wisdom is a defense and money is a defense: But the Excellency of knowledge is that wisdom gives life to them that have it" (Eccl. 7:11–12).**

Obtaining a good understanding is very important. I was personally influenced educationally by Dr. William P. Diggs of Friendship College in Rock Hill, South Carolina. Dr. Diggs is a college professor and Baptist pastor, and was my sociology professor for two semesters at Friendship College. I deeply admired the *God-force* represented in the life of Dr. Diggs, and therefore I followed in his footsteps academically and, based upon his personal recommendation, attended Colgate Rochester Crozer Divinity School. I went to seminary to study the scriptures in depth in order to understand how Jesus lived and to understand through his *examples* how I might be able to love and serve others in Jesus' name: Amen.

Throughout my professional career I did not seek a career in pastoral ministry, but rather taught college-level undergraduate and graduate-level courses in the field of sociology. The information recorded in this book should not be construed as simply a broadbrush indictment of all pastoral leadership. Unfortunately, if there are *ten such pastoral leaders* who fit the mold described in this book operating outside of the *will of God*, it is indeed *ten* too many. God told Abraham that if he could produce ten righteous individuals, he would save the cities; and of course, it is noted in history that Sodom and Gomorrah were destroyed.

On the one hand, I do personally know *some* pastoral leaders who are profoundly double-minded, who simply *preach* and *pray* for money, influenced by greed. It is recorded that you cannot serve two masters: God and *money (or wealth)*. **"For let not that man think that he shall receive anything of the Lord. A double-minded man is unstable in all his ways" (James 1:7–8).** A double-minded individual will invariably say "Lord, Lord," and then appear to be running with the devil. Work is one of

God's gifts to us. New Testament writer Paul says if we do not work, we should not eat. Therefore, if individuals do *any* form of work just for money, they *starve* the soul (the essence of their *being*). On the other hand, I do personally know some pastoral leaders who are profoundly God fearing. I have been a member of Covenant Glen United Methodist Church in Missouri City, Texas, for almost twenty years and Dr. Robert E. Childress is the pastor; Dr. Childress is one such God-fearing pastoral leader.

Pastor Raymond L. Farley of Greater New Sanctuary Baptist Church is a dear personal friend as well as a God-fearing pastoral leader. Dr. John E. Cameron of Greater Mount Calvary Baptist Church in Jackson, Mississippi, is another personal friend and faithful God-fearing servant. Dr. Benjamin Snoddy of Mount Moriah Baptist Church in Spartanburg, South Carolina, is another such God-fearing pastoral leader. I could name others; however, the point is amply made. There is an old saying: "Power corrupts and absolute power corrupts absolutely." Unfortunately, there are too many storefront ministries that have evolved into mega-church ministries that serve only the *founders* of those ministries, not the communities in which they exist. These mega-church ministries give off *"personality-style cult"* impulses, but not real community economic development; they do not demonstrate the old saying: A rising tide lifts all boats. And if not all boats are lifted, if the pastor is the only one in the congregation experiencing prosperity, something is drastically wrong with the picture. Whites by and large join institutional ministries (churches), while minorities by and large follow *personalities.* But again, if in any organization the institutional leader is the only individual prospering, something is wrong with that picture.

In my humble opinion, too many double-minded pastors are using God's name in *vain* for personal *gain*. To be sure, the Israelites were seeking the Promised Land, but today double-minded pastors are erecting Promised-Land Church Monuments—not for people or God, but for self-glorification. The purpose is that they and their extended families might live in Sugar Land and Pearland, shop in Meyerland and ultimately at the "Galleria," and forget about God's hereafter *Promised Land,* which is *heaven*.

While the cities referred to are in the Houston metro area, conceptually and philosophically the process is nationalized. One bothersome question always comes to mind: What's wrong with the church? Could it be that too many pastoral leaders are preaching and praying for brick and mortar? Is it possible that the value orientation of twenty-first century corporate Christianity is too materialistic and, above all, too commercialized? Seemingly the church has become *tax-free capitalism*. The April 2012 issue of *Newsweek* magazine featured an article written by Andrew Sullivan: "Forget the Church: Follow Jesus." The Christian declaration should be: Forget the Capitalistic Corporation: Follow the spirit of God that was in Jesus spiritually reconciling the world—and of course that same *Spirit* is also in each one of us. Mr. Sullivan is absolutely correct in his analysis that *double-minded pastoral leaders* have enslaved Christianity to *corporatism*, to being *money hungry*. This approach is stunting church attendance and spiritual growth.

Many individuals simply do not attend church because the focus is too money centered, not Christ-centered. The *money changers* are back and stronger than ever. The declaration of Sullivan's article is profoundly correct: *Jesus is the church.* Jesus told Peter, "Upon this rock **"I will build my church: And the gates of Hades shall not overpower it" (Matt. 16:18)**. While Mr. Sullivan is right about what is going on in the Christian church community in the name of God, he is absolutely wrong about the solution. The solution is not to forget the church; instead, the solution is to fix the church, thereby fixing the problem. The moral decline of American culture is directly related to the immoral *money-hungry hijacking* of the church by double-minded pastors. Symbols motivate behavior. God desires that the church serve as an eternal symbol of societal moral order, an inward-spiritual consciousness about life. If we fix the church morally we fix society, because the church *must* serve as the moral referee between the good and evil forces in society.

The church then was built upon the *faith* of Peter in the power of God operating in Jesus, and of course, Jesus declared that flesh and blood did not reveal this to Peter. Furthermore, Jesus declared that his kingdom was not of this world; Jesus was not a materialist. In fact, the Jewish people rejected Jesus because they thought he was going to be a *warrior king* just like King David, destroying their enemies and taking over the world. Instead, Jesus taught, **"Love your enemies, bless them that curse you, do good to them that hate you, and pray for them that despitefully use you, and persecute you; that you may be children of your Father which is in heaven: For he makes**

his sun to rise on the evil and on the good, and sends his rain on the just and on the unjust" (Matt. 5:44). Take heed, double-minded pastors: **"Woe to the shepherds who are destroying and scattering the sheep of *MY* pasture, declares the Lord. Therefore, thus says the Lord, God of Israel, concerning the shepherds who are tending *MY* people: You have scattered *MY* flock and driven them away and have not attended to them; behold, I am about to attend to you for the evil of your deeds, declares the Lord" (Jeremiah 23:1–6).** God is saying, even to twenty-first century double-minded pastors, "I see what you are doing: stealing in my name for personal gain."

There is one *double-minded pastor* who has obviously gotten so caught up in the *spirit* of his own namesake that he invites other *double-minded pastors* to dance on money, not dance unto the Lord (it can be viewed on YouTube). King David got drunk, took off his clothing, and danced naked unto the Lord, not unto gold and silver. We might ask the question: What's in a name? Of course, the spiritual power given to Adam in the Garden of Eden was to name everything in creation. How did Adam know that a woman was a woman? He was asleep and didn't have any direct conscious knowledge of the event of her creation, so where did he get the name? Simply put, there is *power* in a name. *Double-minded pastors* are in a competitive personal power struggle with one another, seeking fame and fortune; they are having an *ungodly competition* to determine who is the *greatest,* and they are focused on the power of their own names. The gospel writer Paul's confession ought to be every pastor's confession: "I live by the gospel I preach." Instead the double-minded pastor's message is **"Do as I say and not as I do" (Matt. 18:1–11)**. The test of *greatness* is the willingness to become the lowliest. Jesus participated in a foot-washing service with the disciples in order to illustrate this point (Luke 9:46–48).

If you want to be great, you must be willing to love and serve others; greatness is indeed about love and service. **"For what shall it profit a man, if he shall gain the whole world, and lose his own soul?" (Mark 8:36)**. All of us enter into this physical world with a divine soul, and of course we leave with a divine soul; we also leave a reputation behind. Far too many pastoral leaders seemingly can testify in the *word*, but are unable to walk in the *word* because they have severed their conscience from the *reality of God*. In fact, they have replaced God-consciousness with materialistic things, forgetting that the **"wages of sin is death; but the gift of God is eternal life through Jesus Christ our Lord" (Romans 6:23)**. Double-minded pastoral leaders are always planning the next anniversary celebration (*personalized money-making schemes*) without ever acknowledging that every Sunday they step into the pulpit, it is Jesus' anniversary. These anniversary celebrations are about personal kingdom building rather than *Godly kingdom building*; these celebrations are not about spiritual kingdom building, but rather about a kingdom built by vanity-oriented, carnal-minded men. But, by the grace of God, **"every house is built by some man; but he that builds all things is God" (Hebrews 3:4)**. The double-minded pastor's *implied battle-cry* is: *My church-house is bigger than your church-house*. However, they forget about the *widow's mite* (Luke 21:1–4).

Too many of these double-minded pastors can preach standards of godliness from the pulpit to the laity, but not live up to those same godly standards before the *throne of God* in the world. It is easier for most individuals to look down rather than look up, because we wrestle not against flesh and blood, but confused spiritual leadership in high places. For after all, God sees us before we see ourselves. Pastors need to understand that they are not exempt from the *high calling*. **"For we must all appear before the judgment seat of Christ; that everyone may receive the things done in his body, according to that he hath done, whether it be good or bad. Knowing therefore the terror of the Lord, we persuade men; but we are made manifest unto God; and I trust also are made manifest in your consciences. For we commend not ourselves again unto you, but give you occasion to glory on your behalf, that ye may have something to answer them which glory in appearance, and not in heart" (2 Corinthians 5:10–12)**. *All means all: There are no exceptions to the rule. Without a doubt,* God judges us through Jesus Christ. Pastoral ministry ought to be evaluated by devotion to God through loving and serving others in Jesus' name, and of course God receives the glory.

In fact, to highlight the corporate commercialization of Christianity, in some mega-churches, fast-food restaurants have a prominent commercial presence. In those facilities, there is an *invisible sign* declaring that you can fast-food your way to heaven, rather than declaring that you are what you eat; for after all your body is the *temple of God; therefore, be careful what you eat, especially since food commercialization is not based upon nutritional value but capitalism*. Do not live to eat, but rather eat to live unto God. We know that what we eat is important because there are dietary laws in the Bible.

There are vast differences between the *gospel of Jesus* and the church as a commercialized corporate entity. Jesus said: **"If I be lifted up from the earth, I will draw all men unto me" (John 12:32)**. In Revelation 2:12–14, to paraphrase: God says, I have a two-edged sword. I know your works and where thou dwells, even where Satan's seat is; you hold fast to *my name*, and at the same time deny *my* faith. But I have a few things against thee: you hold the doctrine of Balaam, who taught Balak to cast a stumbling block before the children of Israel to whore after other gods for personal gain and worldly fame.

Corporate Christianity is about material empire building, not soul salvation. Materialism in and of itself denies the interdependence of humankind and therefore lures many misguided individuals into believing that *corporations are people* (as declared by an infamous public figure). Individuals are able to shape the world and to decide their own fate, but could it be that the notion of *rugged individualism* to the exclusion of collective responsibility has caused individuals to neglect their responsibility to the world and each other (*godly stewardship*)? A case in point is the environmental crisis. There are two kingdoms: (1) the kingdom of love, which is collective stewardship or God's kingdom; and (2) the kingdom of power, or politics, which is how individuals work out resource allocation and resource management. The problem associated with resource management is not scarcity, but allocation of the surplus. Although America is *thought* to be a Christian nation, she has kept these two kingdoms virtually completely separated (through the *constitutional separation of church and state: the separation of powers doctrine*). On the one hand, the Christian church has been solely concerned with the God-humankind relationship. On the other hand, politics is concerned with governmental power and corporate money making. As a result, politics in American society has become extremely partisan and divisively toxic, so much so that political governance is becoming virtually impossible. All "-isms" are schisms, and schisms divide rather than unite; but Jesus' way is the only way to life, and life more abundantly.

There is enough to go around; in fact, as stated, the fight is over the surplus. In other words, there is more than enough for a chicken in every pot. The problem is the *will* to share. The needy invariably become the greedy. As a nation we have one vision but different functions. The vision is: "*We hold these truths to be self-evident that all men are created equal . . .*" How we get there is through three distinct governmental functions: *executive, legislative, and judicial;* however, partisan politics about how we achieve the vision is causing untold *mass* societal confusion. Methods and political ideologies have become more important than achieving the vision. The same is true in the religious arena; the division of the church into so many denominations (we could call it *denominationalism*) has become an abomination to God and the church of Jesus Christ. Christianity has one Savior, one vision. The only thing a Christian should understand is the difference between the Old Testament and the New Testament.

On the one hand, the Old Testament is about God acting in the history of the Jewish people for their redemption and salvation based upon *divine law.* On the other hand, the New Testament is about God's grace, mercy, reconciliation, and the gift of forgiveness that comes through the birth, life, death/shedding of blood, resurrection, and ascension of Jesus.

If corporate Christianity is to revive (or *free*) itself and develop a focused moral center, it ought to orient itself towards different values and, above all, restructure its programmatic efforts in order to effectively deal with the urban-suburban complex of social ills we face as a nation. It must therefore reaffirm the *interdependence* of universal humankind and abandon its *corporate* value orientation towards being *money hungry*. But, more importantly, corporate Christianity ought to programmatically address the spiritual issue of how to spiritually strengthen family life in American society, and address the issue of how to make family life creatively more religious. This book focuses its attention on the specific problems of identifying the theology and religion of Jesus, not the theology and religion about Jesus.

The theology and religion of Jesus has three main themes: (1) faithfulness to God, because God is *life (love and service);* (2) collective responsibility and individual cross bearing (*Must Jesus bear the cross alone and all the world go free? No, there is a cross for everyone.*); and (3) setting priorities, or the development of moral character traits. It is my earnest prayer that this book will serve as an *eternal* down payment on a theology of life, a new theology that affirms life as collective responsibility rather than only the notion of life after physical death. One of the thieves on the cross beside Jesus rebuked the other thief for hurling insults at Jesus, and Jesus declared, "*This* day you shall be with me in paradise"—not tomorrow. The life of Jesus was about *agape* love and *selfless* service.

The largest budgetary line-item category in a church's budget ought to be benevolence (home missions, not foreign missions), but instead, in many cases, it is the double-minded pastor's lifestyle living expenses (since they are *self-serving men*): cars, planes, helicopters, yachts/boats, clothing, multi-million dollar homes, and so on. Their motivation for entering the pastoral ministry is personal gain, not love and sacrificial service to others. For many of these *double-minded men,* their sole motivation for entering the pastoral ministry is that it represents the last vestige of respectability, credibility, nobility, and financial security for them and their families' vanity-oriented needs. However, New Testament writer Paul in **Romans 12:2–3** reminds all of us: **"And do not be conformed to this world, but be ye transformed by the renewing of your mind, that you may prove what the Will of God is, that which is good and acceptable and perfect. For through the grace given to me I say to every man among you not to think more highly of himself than he ought, but to think so as to have a sound judgment, as God has allotted to each a measure of faith."** The widows, orphans, blind, lame, and mentally ill are left to fend for themselves. Yet Jesus declared that these are the very individuals that the church is duty bound to take care of. The disciples asked the question: **"When, Lord, did we see you hungry and did not feed you, or naked and did not clothe**

you, or sick and did not visit you, or in jail and did not visit you" (Matt. 25: 35–38)? Jesus' answer to the disciples' questions was: **"Inasmuch as you have done it unto the least of them my brethren, you have done it unto me."** Of course, in Matt. 26:11, Jesus declares that the poor we shall have with us always, but he was referencing the "*poor in spirit*" ***(Matt. 5:3: "Blessed are the poor in spirit, for they shall inherit the Kingdom of God")***, not those who are in physical poverty.

Unfortunately, the *corporate church* is recruiting individuals into becoming lifetime card-carrying members of the walking dead club; individuals who are physically alive but spiritually dead. Double-minded pastors are out of harmony with God and his purposes for the church. Therefore, the purpose of *this book* is to help usher in a more profound sense of accountability, responsibility, credibility, and reliability in pastoral leadership, in terms of God's plan for spiritual kingdom building and soul salvation. *Corporate Christianity* presents a *challenge of faith* to all religious people, be they laity or clergy.

America is facing a serious moral dilemma due to a lack of *spiritual* leadership, *especially Christian leadership.* The moral strength and well-being of family life is directly related to the church, and of course the *family/church partnership* is the spiritual foundation for societal moral order. This moral foundation of family life and church has developed over generations. The solution to America's moral dilemma is in leadership's obedience to God's will and purpose for humankind (*love God and love your neighbor as you love yourself).* Therefore, the solution to our family, church, and societal leadership moral dilemma is and has always been humankind's acceptance of the *reality of God*, because God is Alpha, Omega, and of course everything in between. *God is absolute*, and God has a *universal spiritual purpose* for leadership, not a personal-gain individualistic purpose. Biblical history has taught us this valuable lesson from the Red Sea march of the children of Israel to the civil rights marches of the twentieth century. Of course, some of the marches of the twenty-first century are *insignificant* due to America's moral dilemma.

The cornerstone of social democracy is mass universal education, because democracy is for individuals that can *read, write, and comprehend.* Schools teach values; therefore, the questions are: Whose principles and values are being taught? Are the values universal or particularistic? Do we want everyone enlightened (equal in human dignity) or many individuals left in the dark? No one wants to be *responsible*, especially for sin. For example, consider this question: Who is responsible for bearing and rearing children? Teachers are with our children an enormous amount of time; usually seven hours each school day. On the one hand, teachers cannot be held *primarily* responsible for the moral behavior of the children they teach because moral-behavioral manners, social etiquette, and civility are *values that must be taught and exemplified primarily in the home by parents.* But, on the other hand, teachers do influence value orientations simply because they tend to become role models for children; therefore, they influence values and social behavior by their own *behavioral conduct* in and outside of formal classroom settings. It is no accident but by design that *social conduct* is evaluated on our children's report cards. This of course gives parents valuable information concerning the behavior of their children when they are not under parental influence and direction. Therefore, since teachers have such a profound influence on their students, school leadership must be held accountable as well for children's behaviors and values. Unfortunately, *accountability is measured* primarily through programmatic *entitlement services,* which depend on test scores. So in public education, our children are taught test-taking skills, not how to analytically think—that is, *inductive* and *deductive* reasoning. *God is a logical being* and has created people in his image as logical beings. How to take mandated tests, however, is not about thinking ability, but about *routinizing.* What, then, are the societal effects when institutional leadership fails the individuals that these social and educational programs were designed to serve? While hopelessness and despair abound, the end results are anxiety, frustration, and drug and alcohol abuse.

Society does not need to institute a twelve-step program, but a one-step program towards God. God says, "If you make one step, I'll make *unlimited steps.*" There is no *in between* with God. Jesus says, **"I know your deeds. Therefore, because you are neither hot nor cold I will spit you out of my mouth" (Revelation 3: 15–16)**. God says, **"If my people, which are called by my name, shall humble themselves, and pray, and seek my face, and turn from their wicked ways, then I will hear from heaven, and will forgive their sin, and will heal their land" (2 Chronicles 7:14)**. The *creature/creature-comforts syndrome* has created a mindset of being greater than the Creator *(God),* and of course, the heavenly vision for earthly living is lost because of subliminal messaging—what you see is not what you get. God calls that syndrome into question when he asks Job an important question concerning whether the creature is superior, and God answers with, **"Where were you when I laid the foundations of the earth?" (Job 38:4)**. Job declares that God will deal with the wicked and thus that the Creator is greater than the creature.

Evildoers also frustrated Habakkuk **(Habakkuk 1:2–17)**, and he confronts God out of frustration with a question: **"Lord, how long shall I cry, and thou wilt not hear? Even cry out unto thee of violence, and thou wilt not save? ... Thou art of purer eyes than to behold evil, and canst not look on iniquity: Wherefore lookest thou upon them that deal treacherously, and holdest thy tongue when the wicked devoureth the man that is more righteous than he?"** In chapter 2, God answers Habakkuk's travail. **"And the Lord answered me, and said, write the vision, and make it plain upon tables, that he may run that readeth it. For the vision is yet for an appointed time, but at the end it shall speak, and not lie; though it tarry, wait for it, because it will surely come, it will not tarry. Behold, his soul which is lifted up is not upright in him: But the just shall live by his faith" (Habakkuk 2: 2–4).**

Faith is an action word. A Christian must believe God, trust God, and above all wait on God. If American society is to be *spiritually* healed, humankind must rightfully heed the call of almighty God—even in a highly technologically mechanized culture where one of the important means of mass communication is *texting*. Texting is not a new form of communication, because everything we need to know about life is in a *text*. Consequently, everyone has access to receiving a *divine* text message, for it is recorded in Holy Scriptures from Genesis to Revelation. The Bible is not static; it is a *living word.* **"In the beginning was the Word, and the Word was with God, and the Word was God" (John 1:1–3)**. Of course, the Word (Jesus) became flesh and dwelt amongst us, and we beheld its glory. The Word of God is a living, active word, sharper than any double-edged sword that penetrates and even divides soul and spirit, joints and marrow, and judges the thoughts and attitudes of the heart (Hebrews 4:12).

Double-minded pastoral leaders are leading the way in turning the twenty-first century church into a den of thieves. The church has even been led into accepting bingo, raffling, and other *sordid* money-making schemes. Individuals cannot overcome drinking and gambling without the *Word.* Double-minded pastors are leading churchgoers into believing that they (the pastors) have the "*last word,*" when everyone should know that God has the last word; *thus says the Lord* appears over four hundred times in the Bible. Obviously, far too many pastoral leaders have not heeded this profound declaration, because the Bible is its own reality and therefore brings the reader in direct confrontation with *absolute truth: the reality of God.* Hence, the Bible is not human *speculation* or human *imagination.* The simplicity of the reality of God makes the difference. Therefore, instead of following trends, double-minded pastors *should follow God's instructions in the Word, because the Word works and the world confuses.* The Word works because God is truthful, dependable, and above all authoritatively absolute.

We cannot have peace either in the church house or in the world without moral order. **"For God is not the author of confusion, but of peace, as in all churches of the saints" (1 Corinthians 14: 33).** God structured family in order that he might be included in the social-order fabric of society. How is it that America could be faced with such a breakdown of family life if God is the centerpiece of the church? The answer lies in the fact that *Christian leadership* has missed its *ordination calling* (the mark) in terms of God's spiritual purposes for family life as well as church life. Pastors are not *God. God* is *God.* We all should live by God's Word (*Holy Scriptures*)—pastors as well as laity. No one is exempt from the *commandments* of God. If we talk the talk, we must walk the walk. **"For I rejoice greatly, when the brethren came and testified of the truth that is in thee, even as thou walkest in the truth" (3 John 1:3).** Leadership begins with service, which in turn is God's structure for church and family. Leading mandates *loving* and *serving.*

The experience of salvation and the concept of new birth constitute a laity movement, whereby Christian believers are encouraged to exercise their spiritual gifts as equals before the throne of God. Circumstances, greed, and pastorally-centralized authority have divided churchgoers into classes: clergy and laity. We are all equal in human dignity before God's throne; therefore, division is not biblical. All of us walk through the "*valley of the shadow of death*"; no one is exempt from experiencing physical death, but each individual has a choice concerning spiritual death. The entire Book of Acts and Ephesians 4:11 teach *individual* responsibility to God. The *priesthood* of all believers is paramount in Christian thought; therefore, all individuals have direct access to God and are responsible in ministry to God for our gifts and talents. Unfortunately, the concept of being paid to do *ministry* has led the church into instituting a corporate mentality, and of course the end results are a church house on one corner and the dope house on the other. There is no hope in dope, and seemingly, there is little hope in the church. This is especially true in poorer neighborhoods, which in turn compounds the problem of why the *poor* will always be with us. Simply put, the poor will be both poor in spirit as well as without money; therefore, when the poor receive money, their *value orientation* will not permit them to spend money wisely. Of course, this is not God's intent for humankind. **"But ye are a chosen generation, a royal priesthood, a holy nation, a peculiar people, that ye should show forth the praises of him who hath called you out of darkness into his marvelous light" (1 Peter 2:5–9)**. The history of the church begins with the *creation story* in the Garden of Eden with a *divine purpose* to be fulfilled throughout eternity.

Christian leadership helps to fulfill that purpose and is about a *heavenly vision concerning the soul*, not an earthly vision about storing up materialistic goodies. Jesus always associated the phrase *treasure in heaven* with *moral character and intellectual integrity*. Leadership is about a vision towards the future; indeed the future is children, generation after generation. Of course, there is no such thing as a vision without *God*, because God is the future, and without a vision people perish. **"Where there is no vision, the people perish: But he that keepeth the law, happy**

is he" (Proverbs 29:18). There are two types of individuals in this world: *givers* and *takers*. Deciding which side of the ledger to operate from is about individual choice. **"When the righteous are in authority, the people rejoice: But when the wicked beareth rule, the people mourn" (Proverbs 29:2).** God demonstrated the ultimate form of giving by giving *his* only begotten *Son's* life. **"For God so loved the World that he gave his only begotten Son..." (John 3:16).** How did we inherit this valuable spiritual principle? God gave his very best. Indeed, God gave *himself* for the universal betterment of mankind; therefore, God demands that Christian pastoral leadership give the best, not the rest. A preaching style designed to entertain and solicit emotional impulses from churchgoers is not giving the best, neither to God nor to churchgoers. Emotional expression is appropriate when it is oriented towards *spiritual enlightenment*. It was said of Jesus that he was a *great teacher* sent from God, not a great *whooper* of the world. The greatest sermon that was ever preached is the *Sermon on the Mount* (Matt. 5:1–20). Of course, the Bible declares that when Jesus saw the multitude, he went up onto a mountain, and when he was set, his disciples came unto him and he opened his mouth and *taught* them—not *whooped* at them or entertained them. To be sure, God does not want us to think or act out of emotionalism, but logic.

Biblically speaking, *humankind* is an inclusive concept. Too many twenty-first century Christian pastoral leaders are solely concerned with *me, myself, and I*: they are victimized by the personal pronoun disease. Double-minded pastors are using *"my-ology"* rather than theology as the basis for preaching the gospel of Jesus Christ. As they do, Christianity is becoming an *individualistic corporate money-making entity* that is in competition with the private business sector, while obviously denying the spiritual purpose of the church. It was the Son of God, Jesus, who told his mother at the age of twelve, "You know that I must be about my Father's business, astounding men of knowledge yearning for wisdom." The church is not a business enterprise; *the church is God's spiritual business.* But double-minded pastors are using the Bible as a money-making tool rather than as an instrument of soul salvation. The business of God is soul salvation for all humankind. We have missed the mark of soul salvation, what Christianity really is: The *sinless* conception of Jesus as the only begotten Son of God, and his immaculate birth, life, crucifixion, resurrection, and ascension for the divine forgiveness of sins. **"You cannot serve God and mammon (wealth)" (Matt. 6:24).** For after all, **"consider the work of God: For who can make that straight, which he hath made crooked?" (Eccl. 7:13).** The "god" of this world is money; and therefore the declaration of the world is that every individual has a price. However, the declaration of every Christian believer should be: "I have no price, Jesus paid it all; Glory be to God."

While the church appears to be in disarray, God has promised that the very *gates of hell* shall not prevail against the church. **"For every house is built by some man; but He that built all things is God" (Hebrews 3:4).** For we know that **"except God build the house, they labor in vain that build it: Except the Lord build the city, the watchman waketh but in vain" (Psalms 127:1).**

Indeed, the *cause* of most of our societal ills is lack of *servant leadership* in high places (church and state). Church pastoral leaders today are making *salacious headline stories* and breaking news for unrighteousness (*hoarding*), rather than righteousness. Far too many pastoral leaders are taking the fruits of God's creation primarily for selfish pleasure at the expense of the universal family of mankind. Their message is give, give, give, and give some more. The church of today has gone to the extent of having potential members complete an application to determine where they may fit into the *money-making machine.* It is far too easy for this kind of *exploitation process* to take place within the context of institutional Christianity, because the church has become primarily a middle-class institution, and unfortunately *middle-class* individuals do not really understand the twenty-first century church's agenda; however, they do superficially understand the spiritual role of Jesus. The lines between spirituality and carnality have become so blurred that the average churchgoer cannot differentiate between the two. In twenty-first century America, the factors that motivate pastoral leadership tend to be the same factors motivating American political leadership and corporate business leadership: *storing-up earthly treasure (greed, envy, and jealousy).* With this scenario, in fact, the leadership mentality tends to be flip sides of the same coin. Heads *I* win and tails *I win*; this is a no-win situation for the American people.

The true mission of the church is to *win* souls that are lost unto the reality of God. The church in America, however, has primarily become a middle-class institution, whereby an individual is required to pay to pray; likewise, the secular political world has the philosophy of pay to play (for example, corporate donations). The prerequisite for membership and entitlement to the fruits of the Spirit have become unattainable for many churchgoers because the price tag is too high. Pastoral leadership bases membership recognition upon materialism (measured with personal possessions): houses, cars, clothes, jewelry, and above all money. Too many pastoral leaders are victimized by the same edge-God-out (*EGO*) *plague* that victimizes *most* politicians: power, money, and sexuality (PMS). The children of Israel were affected by plagues that were meant to send a message to Pharaoh: "*Let my people go.*" The message to twenty-first century pastoral leaders is still the same: "*Let my people go*": Free God's people from *worldly bondage* (so they are *in the world but not of the world),* but learn how to hold pastoral leadership accountable. **"But grow in grace, and in the knowledge of our Lord and Savior Jesus Christ. To Him be glory both now and forever" (2 Peter 3:18)**. So be it.

As humans we are duty bound to understand that **"it is written, Man shall not live by bread alone, but by every word that proceeded out of the mouth of God" (Matt. 4:4)**. The plagues that are affecting twenty-first century families are the entirety of social ills that Jesus came to help us overcome. Jesus was an *overcomer* by example. *He* taught that if we do not believe him for what he says, then we should believe him for his works. Jesus was a *servant leader* who *loved* and *tirelessly* served humanity, making all humans equal in dignity before the throne of God as well as in civil society, something that the United

States Declaration of Independence also recognizes: "We hold these truths to be self-evident that all men are created equal and endowed with certain inalienable rights by their Creator." James and John, the sons of Zebedee, approached Jesus in an effort to gain power by *position* rather than love and service, asking for one to sit on his right side and the other on his left side. With power and leadership comes a *cup* of bitter suffering. Who suffers in the power struggle of the church of the twenty-first century? Could it be the next generation?

How do twenty-first century church leaders define power? The answer is: by their ability to have influence with the status quo, by their persuasiveness in the political arena, by having the biggest *money war* chest, and by their ability to influence legislation. Pastoral leaders declare that God *called* them and they are in God's will, but there are no *witnesses*; therefore, we must evaluate them by their *works*. The question is: Are their works *elaborate* church buildings, property development, and affluent personal lifestyles and EGO? For after all, God says, "My kingdom is larger than yours." Without people there is no power. The power struggle is about the needs of people versus profit-making or personal gain. Too many church leaders today are adopting the governance leadership philosophy of the *streets* by becoming *religious pimps*. While the streets should serve as a venue to save sinners (*souls*), they have become passage ways to pimp and influence the weak minded (individuals who are spiritual babies). To be sure, *pimping* should be a social phenomenon associated with whorehouses, not *church houses*. *Religious* pimping is certainly not acceptable behavior in the sight of God and *ought* not to be acceptable behavior to spiritually minded Christians. Jesus was not a self-serving hypocritical personality, nor did he possess a personal gain oriented mentality. In fact, Jesus condemned hypocrites (scribes, Pharisees, and Sadducees). The problem(s) of greed, unemployment/underemployment, children not succeeding in schools, juvenile crime, the breakdown of family life, and so on are all directly related to lack of servant leadership in both the church and state sectors of society. These social issues are only symptomatic of a larger *spiritual leadership* problem. **Ephesians 6:12** says, **"For we wrestle not against flesh and blood, but against principalities, against the rulers of darkness of this world, against spiritual wickedness in high places."** The information presented in this book is *primarily* based upon Holy Scripture. If *any* individuals are offended with the *religious commentary* presented, then argue with the Bible, not the *messenger*. Because **Psalms 1:1–2** says, **"Blessed is the man that walketh not in the counsel of the ungodly, nor standeth in the way of sinners, nor sitteth in the seat of the scornful. But his delight is in the law of the Lord; and in his law doth he meditate day and night."**

The church must abide by God-given laws so that it may be the light of the world. **"Ye are the salt of the earth: But if the salt has lost its savor, wherewith shall it be salted? It is thenceforth good for nothing but to be cast out, and to be trodden under foot of men. Ye are the light of the world. A city that is set on a hill cannot be hid. Neither do men light a candle, and put it under a bushel, but on a candlestick; for it giveth light unto all that are in the house. Let your light so shine before men, that**

they may see your good works, and glorify your Father which is in heaven" (Matt. 5:13–16). Societal laws are manmade, and sometimes manmade laws are in conflict with God-given laws; individuals have the God-given privilege to disobey ungodly laws (we have free will); however, we cannot pick and choose which God-given laws we are willing to obey. Sin is sin. Evil is evil. Disobedience towards God's laws is wickedness. Trust me: God is angry with wickedness every day. Of course there are also rewards for *obedience* every day. Therefore, all of us should live by the fruits of the Spirit, not of the flesh (Gal. 5:22). There is great wrath for disobedience, both personal as well as societal. When we have attained the knowledge of what pleases God, we have reached the highest level of knowing what does not please God. Individuals choose to be in denial and therefore attempt to lie to God by lying to themselves. Be not deceived: God is not fooled nor is he mocked; we reap what we sow (Gal. 6:7). What we see in the mirror is really a *reflection* of ourselves. **"Be not deceived: Evil communications corrupt good manners" (1 Cor. 15:33).** All of us are in a race against time, and the odds are only in our favor when we have the right relationship with God. In the words of Dr. Martin Luther King Jr., "Human progress never rolls in on wheels of inevitability. It comes through the tireless efforts of men willing to be co-workers with God, and without this hard work, time itself becomes an ally of the forces of social stagnation. We must use time creatively, in the knowledge that the time is always ripe to do right."

Let's be clear about it: *lying* is one of the *six things that God hates most of all: a proud look, a lying tongue, hands that shed innocent blood, a heart that devises wickedness, feet that are swift to run to mischief, and false witness that speaks lies, and he that sows discord among brethren* (Proverbs 6:16–17). God hates sin, not sinners. To be sure, fornication is sin, adultery is sin, abortion is sin, homosexuality is sin, men physically abusing women is sin. The three deadly sins are *greed, envy, and jealousy*. One of the overriding problems in twenty-first century America is *greed*. Contrary to popular opinion, greed is not good. There is, though, no need for self-righteousness, be it from clergy, laity, or even (*so-called statesman-like*) politicians. Thus Isaiah says, **"Come now, let us reason together, says the Lord: Though your sins be as scarlet, they shall be as white as snow; though they be red like crimson, they shall be as wool" (Isaiah 1:18). "For by grace are ye saved through faith; and that not of yourselves: It is the gift of God; not of works, lest any man should boast. For we are His workmanship, created in Jesus unto good works, which God hath before ordained that we should walk in them" (Ephesians 2:8–10)**. Again, to reiterate the point, this book is about *spirituality*, not self-righteous social condemnation. In fact, it could be said that this book is a wake-up call to twenty-first century Christianity.

Finally, minority/ethnic communities are in *big* trouble primarily because minorities only have two *primary* institutions: churches and colleges/universities, in addition to the cosmetic commercialized subsidiary industry (hair salons and barber shops). Minority communities suffer severely from the lack of economic opportunities because of structural and spiritual impediments. But minority individuals cannot afford to rob themselves of spiritual principles and moral values in order to obtain material goodies. The lack of *servant leadership* in minority primary institutions has untold consequences and far-reaching developmental implications for both spiritual as well as economic development. Most, not all, of these leadership personalities desire to be *served* rather than to love and serve others. Minority institutions are personality driven rather than community-development driven; they are not given to building and strengthening communities. The evidence of this social fact is most pronounced in minority spiritual institutions (churches), whereby pastoral leaders do not follow church doctrine or church protocol, which is that all things must be done decently and in order. This *truism* is obvious simply by casual observation of the *deplorable plight* of minority neighborhoods and communities; there is usually a church on every corner. This in and of itself is indicative of an institutional leadership problem, because the church is not about physical buildings, but rather *spiritual enlightenment.* In other words, *God's church* is about a building not made by human hands. Could this be the reason why churches on street corners are traditionally referred to as *Pastor Jo-Mo-Blow's Church*? The physical environment in and of itself indicates that things are not done *decently* and in *order*. Additionally, *life*, itself, in minority communities is far too cheap. Individuals physically harm each other all the time. All of this confusion can be directly traced to the breakdown of family structure and family life, and the effects are most pronounced with children. Children are no longer children but have been turned into *kids,* and *kids* are stubborn, disobedient, undisciplined, and hardheaded. A hard head makes for a soft behind, and bad attitudes place bricks on prison walls. As a society, we are probably building more prisons for our children than schools.

What has turned children into *kids* is a *secularized, mechanized, electronic culture:* television, Facebook, texting, Twitter, video games, and so on. Couple this social fact with the deterioration of nurturing, loving, two-parent family structures, and the end results is *kids*, not children who are trained in the way of the Lord. As a result, gangs and peer groups have become surrogate family structures for our children. The church must be willing to shoulder the large *percentage* of the responsibility for this deplorable state of affairs, simply because God intended that churches be about the business of strengthening family life, not making money.

Minority colleges and universities have become *ebony towers,* not ivory towers. They are not institution-building mechanisms that are oriented towards community development; they are indeed *self-serving, dogmatic, and personality driven*; it's the *leadership's way* or the highway. There is virtually no tolerance for dissenting opinion, which is the cornerstone of social democracy. The cornerstone of a university must always be social democracy grounded in spiritual fairness, and spiritual fairness is an ethical concept. A university must always give *respectful expression* to minority dissenting opinion. The concept of majority rule does not mean that the majority is right; it simply means that majority opinion rules. At one point in time only one person was right *(Jesus Christ),* and the entire world was wrong. Of course, Jesus was crucified because he was *right* and the world was wrong. **Exodus 23:1–3** states it plainly: **"Thou shalt not raise a false report: Put not thine hand with the wicked to be an unrighteous witness. Thou shalt not follow a multitude to do evil; neither shalt thou speak in a cause to decline after many to wrest judgment: Neither shalt thou countenance a poor man in his cause...Keep thee far from a false matter; and the innocent and righteous slay thou not: For I will not justify the wicked."**

Without a doubt, the wealthy can *prop* themselves up with money by temporarily relieving the stress of their problems in many sundry ways, while not spiritually resolving their problems. Most individuals who have too much money have a tendency to forget God, and therefore are lured into believing that life is simply about material comfort or wealth. Of course, this is why the most salient value among wealthy individuals is *property rights*. Individuals who do not have enough money to meet basic human needs, however, have a tendency to believe that God has forsaken them and the pain in their lives is too great for them to bear alone; therefore, they rob themselves of spiritual principles and moral values. This is why the poor have the tendency to seek *instant gratification* rather than *delayed gratification*. Even Jesus on the cross, in his humanity, cried out, ***"My God, my God, why hast thou forsaken me?"*** **(Matt. 27:46)**. Since the wealthy tend to forget God and the poor tend to abandon him, in American culture *sustainable values* (values that will take an individual through the good times as well as the bad times) are primarily associated with middle-class values; individuals who do not have too much nor too little, but just enough in order to deal with creative family living. King Solomon declared, "Wisdom is good with an inheritance: And by it there is profit to them that see the sun. For wisdom is a defense, and money is a defense, but the *excellency* of knowledge is, that wisdom giveth life to them that have it." King Solomon is simply saying, Get some wisdom, get some money, but in all of the getting get a *good understanding*, because a *good understanding* is based upon *common sense*—and of course, common sense is not merely common; it is grounded in the reality of God. So be it! And remember that **"no man can serve two masters: for either he will hate the one, and love the other; or else he will hold to the one, and despise the other. Ye cannot serve God and mammon" (Matt. 6:24).** *Money is a cruel master:* No *man* can serve *God* and mammon (*wealth*). Fix the church; fix the problem(s).

I was taught to always get the facts in *black and white*. Therefore, I asked several white pastoral leaders and several black pastoral leaders to review and critique the commentary recorded in this book both spiritually and sociologically. They thought that the information recorded was biblically sound as well as an accurate depiction of what is taking place in many sectors of American Christian society. Unfortunately, there will be many in the black community who will scream loudly that black pastoral leadership is being unfairly criticized. Likewise, there will be many in the white community who will be of the same opinion. Unfortunately, there will be loud screams of unjust characterization on both sides of the Christian equation. My task in writing this book is to shed light on what most Christians already know and understand. God is a God of forgiveness; God gives individuals chance after chance to morally integrate *flesh and spirit*. There is an *old adage*: throw a rock in a pack of dogs, and the dog that barks the loudest is the dog that got hit. The biblical characterization of this *old adage* is recorded in **Matt. 7:15: "Beware of false prophets, which come to you in sheep's clothing, but inwardly they are ravening wolves."** *Corporate Christianity* is about helping to usher in *pastoral accountability* to God, laity, community, nation, and the world community. It is not about black pastoral leadership or white pastoral leadership. In other words, the *commentary* presented is not about institutional racism, but rather about how Christians can usher in *heaven* on earth by doing the will of God as expressed in the life and teachings of Jesus, especially as expressed in the Lord's Prayer. The gospel is not for *sale;* it is a free gift: It is the gift of God through Jesus Christ.

Finally, I have simply had the *moral courage* to write in public commentary what most Christians privately already know to be the truth but will not publicly say. So be it!

Entrepreneurial Christianity

By and large, I have characterized for common-sense purposes the commentary presented in this book about twenty-first century American Christianity as corporate in nature. While for commentary purposes this characterization is convenient, it is not totally an accurate depiction of what really exists. The twenty-first century Christian church has been hijacked by double-minded individualistic self-serving individuals who are employing an entrepreneurial business model under the guise of providing spiritual enlightenment. Entrepreneurial Christianity is strictly an individualistic, vulgar, money-driven business enterprise that is based on ideas, not on soul salvation as God has ordained. A corporation has accountability structures. For example:

- Transparency in operations
- Quality control measures
- A line of authority
- A governance structure, often called the board of trustees

Churches with double-minded pastors often do not have accountability structures. The double-minded pastors want to be accountable to an *invisible God*, not a *real God* that works through and uses people to perfect his will. This has produced individualistic churches, rather than community-based churches that serve the needs of the corporate body of the church and the communities in which they exist.

Without a doubt, it is time for Christian leaders to deal with prophetic teaching and preaching rather than making profits, because the essence of being a Christian is to be Christlike. Jesus was not about profit-making and money-making enterprises. Jesus' ministry was about saving souls.

PRAYER

God of our fathers, by whose grace we are called into *thy divine service* to be under-shepherds in order that *thy* people might be spiritually fed, we bless and honor your *holy* name. We pray that you keep the heart of our minds on how Jesus lived and on your *divine will* as represented in the immaculate conception, birth, life, teachings, death, resurrection, and ascension of Jesus. Make us ever mindful of the words recorded in Micah 6:8: "He hath showed thee, O man, what is good, and what doth the Lord require of thee, but to do justly, and to love mercy, and to walk humbly with thy God?" Fix the *church*; fix the problem(s). God says, "Stop! Look! Listen! The church belongs to my only begotten Son, Jesus Christ; I can and I will fix the church." Amen.

CHAPTER ONE

SNAKEBITTEN: THE GARDEN OF EDEN STORY

The Bible is a historical-spiritual accounting of God acting in human history for the salvation and redemption of humankind. In order to truly understand the Bible, an individual must understand the spiritual chapters in the book of Genesis: chapters 1, 3, 5, 7, and 8. In the Bible, there is only one hero: God. Any other form of hero worshipping is an abomination to God, including apostasy-style preaching. God is not different; he is always the same: absoluteness. The creation of the universe is not out of nothingness, but God establishes order out of chaos. The spirit of God moves upon the face of the waters, and God says, **"Let there be light,"** and there is light **(Genesis 1:1–3)**. God is in everything and touched by nothing.

God in the book of Genesis establishes certain spiritual procedures of order for primary reference, creating moral order, which is connected with peace. That is, God establishes spiritual principles that he will never violate. God never changes and never changes his principles, but because of sin, laws may change. God gives humankind free will, and therefore we are free to become violators of God's principles. We are free to become obedient or disobedient in relationship to the will of God. God is not a dictator of human will or human attitudes towards life. God has given us an exciting collective responsibility for this universe, and therefore we are to become godlike caretakers of the universe. The environmental pollution crisis is a mental and physical disobedience of God's spiritual principles. Thoughts (exploitive ideas grounded in greed) have polluted the air, water, and land. This amounts to a spiritual-mental pollution crisis. The human mind is made up of will, emotion, and intellect. God wants us to think with the logic of our minds—that is, use our intellect. Our souls are housed in our minds. No matter how irresponsible individuals become, God still seeks our highest good. The *destroyer* (the devil) wants us to think with our emotions in order that he might be able to traumatize us about the uncertainties of life. For after all, the *destroyer* wants to kill your flesh, because he knows that he cannot do anything to the spirit of God (*soul*) that is in each of us.

"Therefore leaving the principles of the doctrine of Christ, let us go on unto perfection; not laying again the foundation of repentance from dead works and of faith toward God" (Hebrews 6:1). We should testify to the Word of God, and walk in that Word, and through everything by prayer and supplication with thanksgiving make our request be known to God. That thy will be done in us and through us for others, we humbly pray.

Third John 1:3 says, **"For I rejoiced greatly, when the brethren came and testified of the truth that is in thee, even as thou walkest in the truth."** God told the devil that he could do anything he so desired to Job; except touch his soul/intellect. Again, God wants us to think with our intellect—that is, the logic of our minds, in order that he might speak to us through our conscience. On the one hand, the *destroyer* wants us to think with our emotions in order that he might be able to break us down or have us break out (run from problem solving or blame others). On the other hand, God wants to see us break through to the marvelous light. God is a God of freedom, not equality; he wants us to be free to be what we are in him. That is, to be free to be all that one can be, not equal to be something that an individual can never be, which is another person. God wants us to become overcomers, not leave life to chance occurrences. We are caught up in the dark, deep pits of hell on earth, but we pray to God to help us come out from these pits of hell into his marvelous light. **"If we say we have fellowship with Him, and walk in darkness, we lie, and do not know the truth. But if we walk in the light, as He is in the light, we have fellowship one with another, and the blood of Jesus Christ His Son cleanses us from all sin" (1 John 1:6–7).** Therefore, through faith we must come to the true knowledge that God had his only begotten *Son* die for us that we can, through faith, receive salvation and be born again—to be transformed daily by the renewing of our minds in Christ Jesus. Scripture teaches us that we are to let the mind that was in Christ Jesus also be in us.

The question is, how did we get in the horrible mess that we are in? The answer lies in the Garden of Eden story. The snake bit Adam and Eve, and the poisonous venom passed on through the generational bloodline. **"The carnal mind is enmity against God; for it is not subject to the law of God, neither indeed can it be. So then they that are in the flesh cannot please God" (Romans 8:7)**. The devil influenced the mindset of Adam and Eve towards the flesh (the pleasure principle), because the mind set on the flesh is hostile towards God. Therefore, Adam and Eve became the enemy of God rather than the friend of God. When the spirit of God confronted Adam and Eve with the eternal questions of "Adam, where art thou?" (or "Adam, whose side are you on?") and "Who is it that told you that you were naked?" Adam and Eve immediately sought to *fix* blame rather than take responsibility for their own decisions and actions (disobedience).

Adam blamed Eve, and Eve blamed the devil. In twenty-first century America, we must learn anew to fix the problem(s), not seek to fix blame. The devil didn't make you do it, you did it, and I did it. Let us fully examine what it really consequently meant for Adam and Eve to listen to the devil's voice rather than God's voice. The devil convinced Eve that she would not surely die as God had ordained. Eve then convinces Adam that he would not die. What the devil did not tell Adam and Eve was that the death was not physical, but spiritual separation from God. **"Ye are of your father the devil, and the lusts of your father you will do. He was a murderer from the beginning, and**

abode not in the truth, because there is no truth in him. When he speaks a lie, he speaks of his own; for he is a liar and the father of it" (John 8:44).

What we must remember is that God did not create evil, nor did he create the devil. Everything God created was good. The devil created himself as the *chief opponent of God:* that is, of God's authority over life (heaven and earth). Initially, the devil was a beautiful angel in heaven named Lucifer. God kicked him out of heaven because he challenged God's authority and convinced other angels to rebel against God as well. Moreover, Lucifer (the devil) made false accusations against the Son of God, Jesus. When Lucifer fell to the earth as a fallen angel, he became Satan. Because evil waxed so strong in Lucifer, he transformed himself from Satan into the devil and ultimately the destroyer.

In twenty-first century America, the devil is not some abstract red-looking being with a tail and a pitchfork; the devil just might be a double-minded man. If we analyze the concept of human being, we discover the following. The concept of human is a compound concept involving two words: *hu* (humus) and *man* (mind). God creates a body for man (Adam) made from *humus,* or dirt. God gives man (Adam) his own mind, which is free will. The word *man* means mind. God then breathes the *breath of life* into his nostrils and man becomes a living soul: being = ontology = spirit/soul. Man (Adam) became a living being. The devil is an evil mind; this is why the devil just might be a double-minded man—that is, a split personality halted between two opinions. Without a doubt, we can only judge a tree by the fruit it bears.

God creates this wonderful paradise just for Adam and Eve (universal humanity). Eve was not an afterthought, but a forethought. Everything in the creation was paired. Adam had been placed in the center of the Garden of Eden and given managerial authority over everything in the creation. He (Adam) in fact was the *tree of life*, not a physical tree. God did not breathe the breath of life into a physical tree, but into Adam's nostrils. Trees do not have souls; therefore, God is not concerned with saving trees—that is, God did not breathe the *breath of life* into a tree. God wanted Adam to understand that in order for him to meet the God-humankind *covenant obligation* to him, he would need a helpmeet (*mate*). God wanted Adam to have an "aha" experience when he meets the *woman*, Eve, for the first time. In order that Adam fully comes into the knowledge of the limitations of his authority in relationship to the woman, God places Adam in a *deep* sleep. Therefore, Adam had nothing to do with what took place between God and the woman. Just like Adam, Eve then will have an individual responsibility to God. There is an old secular adage: "Every tub has to sit on its own bottom." So it is with God; every individual soul must give an account for the deeds done in the flesh. For God is so merciful that he will not judge based upon the sins that we committed in the flesh, but the good left undone. Each individual (male or female) has authority over his or her own life decisions.

The power problem in male/female relationships occurs when women use sexuality to gain an advantage over men, and conversely when men use money as power to gain an advantage over women. This circumstance creates a no-win situation for both parties in terms of healthy human interaction, resulting in "thingification," not "human decency." But you cannot beat God at equalizing things. The order in which God creates male and female shows that their interactions were not intended to be about gaining an advantage over each other, but for their mutual benefit and for them to know love. Adam is placed in a deep sleep, and he has nothing to do with the making of a woman. God takes a rib from Adam's side and forms the woman, Eve. Now, because he is short of a rib, Adam is incomplete without Eve. When Adam wakes up, there is this beautiful woman standing before him, and he says, **"Aha" (Genesis 2:21–25)**. Eve asks Adam, Who are you? Adam answers, I am man. Eve asks, Who am I? (This reveals an identity issue—she is interdependent on Adam to know who she is.) Adam answers, You are bone of my bone and flesh of my flesh; you shall be called woman.

Keep in mind during this entire episode Adam has been unconscious and has had nothing to do with God's work of making a woman. His knowledge is purely spiritual knowledge of what took place while he was sleeping, not flesh-experience knowledge. The word *woman* means *one man*. God performs the first marriage ceremony: Adam and Eve, not Adam and Steve. We can rightly say that marriage ought to be a holy sacrament of the church, not civil courts (society). Marriage then is of God, for God, and above all for children. Therefore, one plus one according to God and Adam in marriage does not equal two, but, as Adam stated, it equals one.

Now the devil (the destroyer) and the snake have the same tricky, subtle characteristics (nature). Since the devil is a spirit, he needs a physical body in order to perfect his will (Genesis 3:1–24). Therefore, the spirit of the devil enters the physical body of the snake. The devil using the body of the snake engages Eve in a *power struggle conversation* about God's authority and Adam's stewardship (managerial) responsibility. The devil tells Eve, "*Woman,* let me tell you something that God does not want you to know about power—that is, about the power of sexuality. You have the power! You do not have to listen to Adam or God. God does not want you to be as *wise* as *he* is, and of course you know that the man, Adam, does not want you to be equal to him. Adam wants to rule over you. God lied to you and Adam. If you eat, you will surely not die. I can show you what God did not want you to know. "

The *destroyer* is the author of lies; he is a liar, and the truth is not in him. What Eve found out too late was that the death was spiritual, not physical. The death was *spiritual separation* from God. Sin creates spiritual separation from God, because God hates sin. Satan says, "*Woman,* I am a real friend; don't you know that you can look up longer than Adam can look down? Of course, if you get him looking down, then he will not look to the hills from whence cometh his help, and think that all of his help comes from the Lord, who made the heavens and the earth. *Woman (girlfriend)*, you can really trust what I am saying; you can get Adam to think that what you can do for him is all he needs. Adam does not have any authority over you; trust me, you can get Adam to do anything you want him to do. Do you really want me to show you how? Do you really want me to show you where the real power lies?"

The devil was talking about the power of human sexuality, because sexuality is God's gift to us, when dealt with appropriately. The devil tells Eve, "Neither God nor Adam wants you to be *equal* to them." The one thing the devil did not tell Eve was that we cannot beat God equalizing things. God's issue for humankind is not equality but *freedom* of choice (free will—God gives us freedom of conscience to make our own choices about how we live). Trust *me,* the devil cannot tell the truth; and of course the devil's *issue* is not freedom, but *slavery.*

As human beings, we must learn how to deal with freedom (*free will*). God creates a man from the dirt and breathes the breath of life into him. God creates a woman from a man, and the man had nothing to do with the making of the woman. To be sure, everybody that is born into this world must come through the womb of a woman, because the womb of a woman symbolizes the Garden of Eden: that life is a free gift. Indeed, a baby in its mother's womb has life as a *free gift* with no struggle. The baby's struggle comes at birth and thereafter.

When we do not use our free will in a godly way, God will equalize our choices; he will set things straight. God is a God of freedom and free will; the devil puts individuals in bondage, because the devil has a *graveyard* mentality. The beauty of God's work is what we invariably can learn about motherhood. There are three mothers: mother earth, man, and woman. The mother of Adam was the earth. This is why we affectionately refer to the earth as mother earth, but modern societies because of greed have not taken care to treat our mother with the respect that she deserves—case in point, the environmental crisis.

Adam was the mother of Eve. Therefore, men need to learn how to nurture women. Women are the mothers of children, and therefore they have to learn how to teach children to love their fathers, but most of all they must learn how to *father* men. Women need to learn how to strengthen men in order that they might learn how to meet their obligations to God, family, and community/country.

The devil then shows Eve what human sexuality is all about. We do not know how long the devil had been having sex with Eve, but we do know that the devil did have sexual intercourse with her. Indeed, it is not an accident of human history that down through the ages the *snake* is the symbol most often used in sex-cult activities. We know that the devil had sexual intercourse with Eve by the nature of the conversation that took place between God, Adam, and Eve (Genesis 3). The devil needs a *host (body)* in order to perfect his *destroyer* will, because he is a spirit. Therefore, the devil is not like God who is omnipresent, in everything but touched by nothing. We also know that historically prostitution is the oldest profession known to humankind and that God *hates* prostitution, and of course we know why. You cannot sell love (*agape*). Sexuality should be an expression of divine love (agape) between a man and a woman. That is, God intended that sexuality be an expression of love, not lustfully flesh oriented towards pleasure-seeking vanity. You cannot sell that which is of God; this is why Jesus chased the money changers out of the temple. The church should be a temple of love.

The spirit of God comes back into the Garden of Eden, because God sits high and looks low. The psalmist in **Psalms 139** refers to the inescapable presence of God. **"Lord, thou hast searched me and known me. Thou understand my thoughts afar. Thou hast beset me behind and before. Whither shall I go from thy spirit? Or whither shall I flee from thy presence? If I ascend up into heaven thou art there: if I make my bed in hell, behold thou art there. If I take the wings of the morning, and dwell in the uttermost parts of the sea . . . Even there shall thy hand lead me, and thy right hand shall hold me."** Jonah sought to escape the will of God, and God placed him in the belly of a "big" fish—and he arrived at God's destination for his life a day earlier than originally intended.

God asked Adam, "Adam, where art thou?" This question is about loyalty and leadership. Adam, what are you doing: following or leading? In other words, Adam, whose side are you on? I left you in charge. Adam answers by saying, "I am hiding." God says, "Why are you hiding?" Adam answers, "I am hiding because I am naked." God says, "Who told you, you were naked?" Sin will make us hide not only from God, but from one another. Adam answers, "The woman that you gave to me did give to me to eat, and I did eat." Indeed, the apple of a man's eye is a woman. The apple on the tree is the pear on the ground. My Christian friends, believe me, they are not talking about eating apples. God said, "Do not mess with the apples" before it is time to eat. A *baby* should not eat an apple before it is time; its digestive system cannot handle it.

Adam and Eve were physically naked all the time. So what type of nakedness was Adam referencing? I submit that Adam was referencing nakedness of mind, or the loss of sacredness between God and himself because of his disobedience. The devil had influenced Eve to live by the flesh (power of sexuality/pleasure principle), and Eve convinced Adam to live by the flesh. Remember that the objective of the devil is to rob, steal, and kill—to destroy the flesh, because your soul belongs to God. The *blame game* was birthed in the Garden of Eden. Adam said, "The woman that you gave me did give to me to eat of the tree, and I did eat." Remember, man is the tree of life, not a physical tree. It, indeed, was man who was placed in the center of the Garden of Eden, not a physical tree. "And God said unto the woman, what is this that thou hast done? And the woman said, the serpent beguiled me, and I did eat." The destroyer tricked me, and of course, from that day until the present time, many women have decided to turn *tricks.* Prostitution is indeed the oldest profession. But God hates prostitution, because love is of God; it is freely given.

Sexuality and love are not the same. God's plan was for love and sexuality to be morally integrated. The devil's plan was for the two to be separated in order to create confusion, and of course the devil, in part, has succeeded. God said to the serpent, **"Thou art cursed, and dust shalt thou eat all the days of thy life. I shall put enmity between thee and the woman and between thy seed and her seed" (Genesis 3:15)**. If this is not a reference to *sexuality,* I must not be able to read and comprehend.

Then God says to the woman, **"I will greatly multiply thy sorrow and thy conception, in sorrow thou shalt bring forth children, and thy desire shall be to your husband, and he shall rule over thee" (Genesis 3:16)**. Again, if this is not referring to sexuality, I must not be able to read and comprehend. Then God says to Adam, **"Because you have listened to the voice of your wife, and eaten of the tree that I commanded you not to eat of, cursed is the ground for thy sake" (Genesis 3:17)**. Adam, you are going to have to *work,* ***"thorns and thistles you shall have,*** **all the days of your life. By the sweat of thy face shall you eat bread until you return unto to the ground, because you came from dirt and to dirt shalt thou return" (Genesis 3:19).**

Without a doubt, the devil's snakebite venom in the Garden of Eden oriented humankind towards the pleasure of the flesh (sexuality)—the most pleasurable part of human existence—rather than towards the spirit of God. Individuals seek to maximize pleasure and minimize pain. To the casual observer, there is untold sexual confusion in American society as well as in the world community. In fact, there is an international capitalistic sex-trafficking mafia. The sexual confusion in the world community is charged to the children of the world to the *nth* degree.

Marriage is of God; it is instituted of God for divine spiritual purposes. Marriage is both for God and humankind; spiritual and physical in nature—that is, both for spiritual (soul salvation) as well as physical immortality (children heritage). This is why Sarah the wife of Abraham *cried* out to God, declaring, "Give me children or else I *die.*" Of course, Sarah did not have *faith* that God could perfect *his will* in her life, even when she was old and beyond childbearing years. Nothing is impossible for God if we believe and have *faith*, because it is faith that moves the hand of God. God told Adam and Eve to be fruitful and multiply and replenish the earth (Genesis 1:28). In Genesis 2:24–25, God establishes the fourfold foundation for marriage: the law of priority (prove these things); the law of pursuit (cleave to each other); the law of possession (your body does not belong to you); and the law of purity (sin is a hindrance to purity-righteousness). Marriage is a *covenant-obligatory* relationship essentially for the procreation of children (physical immortality); therefore, marriage is for children, not adults, because adults want to be *footloose* and *fancy free*.

Eve is the bride symbolizing the church, just as Jesus is the church. **"Men ought to love their wives as their own bodies. He that loves his wife loves himself. For no man ever yet hated his own flesh; but nourishes and cherishes it, even as the Lord the church" (Gal. 5:28–29)**. If God's spiritual plan of salvation for the soul and physical immortality for human beings is marriage and family, and of course, children are the physical-spiritual reflection of that purposed plan, what then is the *societal rancor* concerning same-sex marriage? There are two spiritual powers in this world: God and Lucifer (the devil). The only *spiritual power* that wants legalized sin is *Lucifer, not God*.

I submit that the *ungodly* conversation concerning same-sex-marriage is, to say the least, *utter nonsense*. God does not violate *his commandments/principles*, but *we as a society* have the free will to do so. But, on the other hand, as Christians we must reject *Caesar's* attempt to institute same-sex marriage into law. God says that he gives homosexuality over to a reprobate mind. **"And even as they did not like to retain God in their knowledge, God gave them over to a reprobate mind, to do those things that are not convenient, being filled with all unrighteousness, fornication, wickedness, covetousness, maliciousness, full of envy, murder, debate, deceit, malignity; whisperers, backbiters, haters of God, despiteful, proud, boasters, inventers of evil things, disobedient to parents . . ." (Romans 1:21–32).** Individuals have a *human right* to participate in homosexuality (same-sex sexuality); no one knows what goes on behind closed doors. Sexuality is private business, not public opinion. No one seeks *third-party* permission to experience sexuality, whether homosexual, heterosexual, fornication, or adultery. Therefore, homosexuality is a human right, not a *civil right*. The ontological concept of God concerning sexuality defies anthropological characterization.

When Adam and Eve disobeyed God's command, and the apple on the tree became the pear on the ground, they covered their private anatomy with fig leaves. Adam and Eve covered the parts of their bodies that violated God's command. God then covers Adam and Eve with lambskin, symbolizing that sexuality is a *closed-door, private-business experience, not a public-business open to everyone's opinion*. God is asking us the question: What is this ungodly (*destroyer-devil*) conversation concerning same-sex marriage really about? Maybe it is about the children—that is, since two men cannot reproduce through homosexuality, nor can two women reproduce through homosexuality. In the first instance, homosexuality is a male phenomenon anyway—that is, women experience *nothing* different with another woman that they cannot experience with a man; they are simply *playing* with each other. Obviously, this is not true with two men: I know that the reader understands the drift of the commentary.

This is why homosexuality is people turning inward to become lovers of themselves, seeking to serve their own EGO (Edge God Out) interests. Life is not about having a good time all the time; there must be some *redemptive suffering* sometime. No pain, no gain. Consequently, when individuals who practice homosexuality physically die, their homosexual activities die as well. But glory to God: a man and a woman can reproduce their kind, because their statuses are male and female, and God created them male and female. Homosexuality is sexual activity, just like heterosexuality is sexual activity; it is not a status.

Marriage is not just about human relationships; it is also about God's spiritual purpose that is directly related to procreation or children. Marriage is a covenant relationship, not a contractual relationship, similar in nature to the covenant relationship that God established between *himself* and humankind. Without a doubt, there are two issues that the Christian church should never embrace: *same-sex marriage* and *abortion*.

Authentic Christianity cannot and should not become *cultural Christianity*, as many double-minded pastors are seeking to have it become. If the church becomes a mirror reflection of secular culture, then it ceases to be the authentic church of Jesus Christ that Jesus referenced when referring to Peter's *faith*. It is obvious to the casual observer that the *Flip Wilson* declarative statement about the devil is not working; only the *Word* works, when it is implanted in the minds of individuals. "Let the mind that was in Christ Jesus be also in you" should be the *Christian battle cry*. **"What shall we then say to these things? For if God be for us, who can be against us?" (Romans 8:31).** For **"if ye continue in my word, then are ye my disciples indeed; and ye shall know the truth and the truth shall make you free" (John 8: 31).** God said, "I have heard thee in a time accepted, and in the day of salvation have I succored thee: Behold, now is the accepted time; behold, now is the day of salvation." *Flip Wilson* was a popular comedian who was famous for popularizing the phrase, "*the devil made me do it.*" The devil might have influenced our actions, but we chose the action because individuals have free will. God is saying that the devil might have influenced us to violate *his* commandments, but he is going to do a *new thing* just for us; by grace we are *forgiven* through the birth, life, death, shedding of blood, resurrection, and ascension of his Son, Jesus Christ.

Individuals were created for greatness. God created man, male and female, in his own image, in the image of God created he them (Genesis 1:27). The image of God is spiritual, not anthropological. This is why institutional racism is such a *sinful* affront to the reality of God. Racism is a *twisted and confused* amoral judgment about universal humanity. How can we say that we love God whom we have not seen and cannot see, and hate our fellow man? Looking at skin color rather than character and integrity is an abomination to God. None of us created ourselves or chose our parents. God says he knew us before we were conceived in our mother's womb, even the number of hairs on an individual's head. Of course, everything God created was good. Spiritually, the snakebite in the Garden of Eden started human history out on a live-by-the-flesh (let's have a party; good times are here forever), destructive, pleasure-principle journey. God is eternal cause and humankind is effect. The book of Genesis is about God, not the creation. In the creation story, God implicitly gives the first commandment: "Thou shalt have no other gods before me" (idolatry). Therefore, in the creation story, humankind is confronted with two overriding dilemmas: (1) the issue of idolatry, which raises the question, Who do you love the more, the Creator or the creation? and (2) humankind's collective social identity—godlike, but not God. Herein lays the paradox of human existence—godlike, but not God.

To review, God creates all things for humankind, and then he creates man (Adam and Eve) for himself. Eve is not an afterthought; God wanted Adam to realize that he needed help (a *helpmeet)* in order to meet his divine obligation to God. God gave us a real world, but we have created an *unreal* world made up of phony unrealities. The evidence is profoundly displayed in our theological approach in our churches, our politics, our popular culture, and above all in our individual lifestyles. No matter how hard we try to confuse God's real world, God is constantly recreating and intervening, making it anew through his Son's resurrection and ascension (divine intervention). God used Abraham, he used Moses, he used King David, and he used Jesus his only begotten Son to *recreate* the moral integration of flesh and spirit. Spiritual schizophrenia is a deadly disease and hazardous to our soul salvation. For this cause I bend my knees unto God the Father, of whom the family of humankind is named, that God would grant us, according to the riches of his glory, *time* to become obedient and faithful children of God. For **"blessed are the peacemakers: for they shall be called the children of God" (Matt. 5:9)**. However, peace without moral order is not peace.

PRAYER

God of our Fathers, we know that what is God to some is the devil to others. We know that Jesus belongs to the world as well as the *ages*, because he came from heaven to renew the minds of individuals through faith unto salvation that we might be spiritually born again. Teach us, Father God, how not to become irresponsible children of children, telling each other the destroyer's (devil's) lies. We pray as Christians that others might see our good works and come running to ask, "What must I do to be saved?" Because as Christians we are the light of the world. Fix the *church*; fix the problem(s). God says, "Stop! Look! Listen! The church belongs to my only begotten Son, Jesus Christ; I can and I will fix the church." Amen!

CHAPTER TWO

A SOCIO-THEOLOGICAL ANALYSIS OF THE COVENANT

Double-minded pastors need to stop brainwashing churchgoers into believing that being identified with them is the only way to understand the reality of God and to go to heaven. There is a great possibility that by dealing with double-minded pastors, we are already in *hell*, because they are creating heaven on earth for themselves while having us operate under the illusion that they are serving God. Double-minded pastors know that they are not serving God, but serving self. God is a universal God: He does not leave *any* of his children in this world as *unproductive* fools. Every individual can understand the personal covenant relationship that God has with each *soul*. God obligates himself first to each individual before he expects us to obligate ourselves to him.

"But as it is written, eye hath not seen, nor ear heard, neither have entered into the heart of man, the things which God hath prepared for them that love Him" (1 Cor. 2:9). We do not have to go to a double-minded pastor in order to understand how much God loves us. Reading John 3:16 will readily give us that information. Of course, **John 3:17** makes it clearer: **"For God sent not His Son into the world to condemn the world; but that the world through Him might be saved."**

In the beginning, the spirit of God moved upon the face of the deep, and what was chaos then became a harmonized world (Genesis 1:2). God is God, and everything else is created. Adam and Eve confused their real-world stewardship roles with that of God's divine authority. God created humankind for his divine glorification; not himself for humankind. This confusion on the part of Adam and Eve of outward appearance with inward reality was the beginning of the process of instituting irresponsibility (what we would call *rugged individualism)* as a social value. Adam and Eve defied God's reality in order to create their own unrealities, rather than submit to God's truth about human interdependence. Adam and Eve wanted to become their own god, or wanted to become slaves to another god. The spiritual fall of Adam and Eve in the Garden of Eden was the beginning of humankind's love affair with lies (unrealities), rather than God's divine truth. God is God because he knows how to love and serve. Man is man because he wants to be served. A *god* ought to serve others and not be self-serving. If he does not, then he loses the loyalty of his servants. Indeed, servant leadership is about serving others, not self-centeredness.

Could it be that this is a profound lesson that many double-minded pastors need to learn? Of course, a self-serving life is always a self-defeating life. Jesus declared that those who seek to save their lives invariably lose their lives (which is the cost of discipleship). **Matt. 4:19** says, **"Follow me, and I will make you fishers of men."** To be sure, Jesus' declaration is about saving lives, not acquiring personal wealth and erecting *mega-church complexes* as personal *competitive* monuments to foolish pride. Humans are humans because they want privileges without responsibilities; individuals want to be served, rather than to serve. The notion of *rugged individualism* starts the world off on a dangerous negative collision course. Case in point: the Cain and Abel story (Genesis 4:1–16). Allow me to paraphrase the story: Abel gives God his best and Cain does not. God asks Cain, "Why you are looking towards the ground?" In other words, why has your countenance fallen? Why not look to the hills from whence cometh all your help? If you do well and do not let sin lay at your door, you will be accepted. Cain becomes jealous and kills his brother, Abel. And God says unto Cain, "Where is your brother?" Cain lies to God. He answers, "I don't know; am I my brother's keeper?" God says, "I hear your brother's *blood* crying from the ground." Cain is banished and declares that his punishment is too great; nowhere in the Bible is it recorded that Cain dies. The spirit of evil that was in Cain is still wreaking havoc on the earth. As humans multiplied, so then did evil and unrighteousness.

Genesis 6:3 says, **"My Spirit shall not strive with man forever, because he is also flesh; nevertheless his days shall**

be one hundred and twenty years." "And God said unto Noah, the end of all flesh is come before me; for the earth is filled with violence-through men, and behold, I will destroy them with the earth" (Genesis 6:13). "But with thee will I establish my covenant" (Genesis 6:18). God condemns the unrighteousness of individuals and moves to recreate interdependence and harmony in the universe by establishing a covenant with Noah. The principle of individualism has always distorted the world that God envisioned for humankind. Noah's faith and righteous obedience to the *will of God* becomes his invitation to join God's liberating and recreating activity in the world. God used a political event *(the great flood)* to alter the course of human history (Genesis 7:17–19). God does not separate life into categories; life is life, and there is only interdependence. Individualism causes men to want to remake the world into their own egoistical images. As stated in chapter one, *EGO* is an acronym for *Edge God Out.* When individuals do not value life but value the "gun" as the basis for conflict resolution, then there is no basis for human community. Wars and rumors of wars shall prevail.

EGO is a deadly disease because it causes individuals to safeguard privileges, rather than to share responsibilities and sacrifices. God's covenant relationship with Noah is about faith, because without faith it is impossible to please God. Sin is spiritual separation from God. **"For the wages of sin is death, but the free gift of God is eternal life in Christ Jesus our Lord" (John 6:23).** The covenant process begins with Noah and is sealed with Abraham and renewed with Isaac. Isaac receives the *covenant* promise. Ishmael receives the *blessing:* the gift of Middle Eastern oil. God promises to multiply Abraham's seed exceedingly (Genesis 17:1–11). The covenant is about reestablishing the principle of human interdependence, which, in turn, had been eroded by Cain's declaration, "*Am I my brother's keeper?*" In God there is no question of merit. The arrogance and pride of the Jewish people sought to reduce the covenant to privilege. God had already declared in **Genesis 12:3, *"In you all of the families of the earth shall be blessed."*** This verse of Scripture is the foundation of the covenant with Abraham. The Israelites were called to be the example of righteousness in which the will of God was made known to people(s) through their obedience to God. This notion of the covenant has long since been forgotten. In the twenty-first century, the foundation of modern Judaism is consciously grounded in ethnic identity. Historically, an individual could through circumcision be incorporated into the people of Abraham—which is the divine covenant. Today you are not Jewish unless your mother is Jewish. Therefore, individuals who wish to convert to Judaism in modern times face almost insurmountable obstacles.

It seems, in order to have a legitimate share in the blessings promised Abraham, the qualification is racial ethnicity. The social history of the Jewish people, while it bound them together, has served as an alienating factor in the human experience. The Maccabean Wars were attempts on the part of some Jews to break down this wall of alienation. It has been this *wall* (*chosen ones*) that time and time again aroused the violence of other nations against Jewish people. For after all, Jewish exclusivism in recorded scriptures has no basis in God's reality. All of the social, political, and economic barriers that alienate individuals are concentrated in this complex division between Jew and Gentile. To God, the covenant represents human interdependence. But to the Jewish people, the covenant meant exclusivity; non-Jews were outside the law and, above all, outside of the promise of God. It is for this reason alone (exclusivism) that Judaism is known as the non-proselytizing religion. In other words, you are not Jewish unless your mother is Jewish; ethnic birth is determinative, not religious conviction.

To be sure, the whole world, with or without the law, is collectively guilty before God. **"For as many as have sinned without law shall also perish without law: And as many as have sinned in the law shall be judged by the law; for not the hearers of the law are just before God, but the doers of the law shall be justified" (Romans 2:12–13)**. The Old Testament history books (1 and 2 Chronicles) clearly depict in the social history of the Jews how utter disaster results when a "*peculiar*" people abandon God. The Jewish people consistently forgot to ***"fear God and keep His commandments: For this is the whole duty of man"*** **(Ecclesiastes 12:13)**. The *great flood* was simply a political reminder of God's divine authority over life. Without a doubt, it was soon forgotten. Humankind's memory is, indeed, very short. We are slow learners, and history reveals that we have not learned very much at all about spiritual life, even in the twenty-first century. In **Romans 8:7–12**, God says, **"The days are coming when I will establish a new covenant with the house of**

Israel and with the house of Judah: not like the covenant which I made with their fathers." The Jewish people were not faithful in the original covenant. God, therefore, gives us a better covenant in Jesus Christ (the Righteous One). God says that He is going to remove forever the sting from death and victory from the grave. For the wages of sin is death, but the gift of God is eternal life through Jesus Christ our Lord (Romans 6:23). For if we live by the flesh rather than the Spirit, we are already dead. For the mindset of the flesh is death, but the mindset of the Spirit is life and peace, because the mindset of the flesh is hostile towards God; for it does not subject itself to the law of God, for it is not even able to do so, and those who are in the flesh cannot please God (Romans 8:6–8). **"But without faith it is impossible to please Him: for he that comes to God must believe that He is, and that He rewards them that diligently seek Him" (Hebrews 11:6–39).**

By faith Noah, being warned of God of things not yet seen, moved without fear. . . . By faith Abraham, when he was called to go out into a place, obeyed; and went out, not knowing whether he went. By faith Moses, when he was born, was hid for three months by his parents because they saw that he was a proper child and they were not afraid of the king's commandment. Simply put, faith is the substance of things hoped for and the evidence of things unseen. It is faith that pleases God. God, therefore, because of the faith of our fathers, removed the covenant of death from us since the wages of sin is death, and established a new covenant through the birth, life, death, resurrection, and ascension of Jesus Christ.

PRAYER

Lord, teach us to keep faith with the covenant that you made with our forefathers to forgive us of our sins (transgressions) in order that our souls might be at peace. But, more importantly, help us to receive the ministry of *Christ Jesus*, who is the mediator of a better covenant and a better promise because *Christ Jesus* is faultless. Purge our conscience from dead works to serve the living God. Fix the *church*; fix the problem(s). God says, Stop! Look! Listen! The church belongs to my only begotten Son, Jesus Christ; I can and I will fix the church. Amen!

CHAPTER THREE

WHAT DO YOU THINK ABOUT JESUS?

Jesus asked the Pharisees this question: What is your opinion of Jesus Christ, the Righteous One? What do you think of Jesus? Sooner or later every discussion of religion leads to this question. In the end, in some manner, all of us are going to encounter the life of Jesus Christ. The question is inevitable and inescapable. Our individual answers might be different from the church's answer. Jesus has been called a prophet, a poet, a psychologist, a great teacher sent from God, and the Son of God. All individuals have an interest in knowing who Jesus is, even though they may not be aware of this fact. Every tongue must confess and every knee must bow: **"For there is one God, and one mediator between God and men, the man Christ Jesus, who gave Himself as a ransom for all, the testimony *borne* at the proper time" (1 Timothy 2:5–6)**. Without a doubt, Jesus Himself thought that this was an important question. The question of the identity of Jesus is inescapable because it is an eternal question. **"It is a trustworthy statement, deserving full acceptance, that Christ Jesus came into the world to save sinners, among whom I am foremost of all" (1 Timothy 1:15).**

Double-minded pastors should embrace the testimonial declaration of Timothy. They have failed miserably in their misguided efforts towards helping Christian believers understand the spiritual role of the birth, life, death, resurrection, and ascension of Jesus in relation to sin, forgiveness, and soul salvation. Double-minded pastors have been so busy raising money for bigger church houses and *phony* worldly lifestyles (personal kingdoms) that they have neglected to tend to the souls of churchgoers and the benevolent needs of the communities in which they exist. All this *unrighteous-mess* is oriented towards the nemesis of the disciples James and John (Matt. 18:1–11): Who is the greatest in the kingdom of God? God's answer comes in **Matt. 20:16: "So the last shall be first and the first shall be last: For many are called, but few are chosen."**

There is a profound reason why the gospel of Matthew begins with the genealogy of Jesus physically and spiritually—simply put, because Jesus primarily came from the lineage of ancestors who knew God, called upon God, served God, and lived in the will of God. **"But these are written, that ye might believe that Jesus is the Christ, the Son of the Living God; and that believing ye might have life through His name" (John 20:31). "And this is life eternal, that they know thee the only true God, and Jesus Christ, whom thou have sent" (John 17:3).** Without a full and complete understanding of the life, death, shedding of blood, resurrection, and ascension of Jesus, as humans we cannot begin to understand what God intended us to become. To be sure, God wants us to become more like him by loving and serving others. Double-minded pastors in their corporate greed have spiritually and morally bankrupted the church; these double-minded pastors have made themselves the church, and churchgoers have simply become the pawns of corporate church success. Jesus asked Peter the question, "Who do men say that I am?" Peter replied, "Thou art the Christ, the Son of the Living God." Jesus replied, "Flesh and blood did not reveal this to you." Jesus is the measuring rod (standard of measurement) for who we are as humans, and above all for what Christianity can be and ought to become.

"Verily, verily I say unto you, he that heareth my word, and believeth on Him that sent me, hath everlasting life, and shall not come into condemnation, but is passed from death into life" (John 5:24). If we do not want to retain God-consciousness in our minds, God will give us over to a reprobate mind: "For the invisible things of *Him* from the creation of the world are clearly seen, being understood by the things that are made, even His eternal power and Godhead; so they are without excuse." Jesus declared, "Think not that I am come to destroy the law, or the prophets: I am not come to destroy but to fulfill." How Jesus lived, how he died, and above all how God raised him from the dead fulfills the law and the faith and work of the prophets. Even in twenty-first century America pleading ignorance of the law is no excuse; "sorry" is still a sorry word. Jesus belongs to the world (universality), and as Christians, we belong to Jesus.

Because of his faithful obedience to God, Jesus was given a name above all names: *Christ, the Righteous One*. Joseph's family name was not Christ. The name *Christ* assures us that Jesus is the victor. God was in Jesus reconciling the world unto him and us unto each other. When we entrust ourselves into God's care we meet Jesus, through the divine action of the Holy Spirit. **"Therefore if any man be in Christ, he is a new creature: Old things have passed away; behold, all things have become new. And all things are of God who hath reconciled us unto Himself by Jesus Christ, and hath given to us the ministry of reconciliation" (2 Cor. 5:17–18).** Jesus is what's new and Jesus is what's old. In order to live life creatively an individual must have an encounter with Jesus. The question is: Have you had an encounter (rendezvous) with Jesus? Have you met Jesus at the crossroads of your life? Have you met Jesus in the garden? Every individual at some point in time must come to grips with how Jesus lived, because it was how Jesus lived that enabled him to die in the will of God. Jesus was the bearer of the kingdom of God; he is God's agent.

God demands perfection from all of us. We can be perfect, and of course, individuals are perfect when they realize the reason for their creation. Jesus said that there are two things individuals must have: (1) an awareness of the reality of God and (2) faith, because faith is an action concept that helps us create an encounter with God. **"So then faith cometh by hearing, and hearing by the word of God" (Romans 10:17). "Now faith is the substance of things hoped for, the evidence of things not seen" (Hebrews 11:1).**

Jesus proclaimed that **"the Spirit of the Lord is upon me, for He has anointed me to preach the gospel of good news to the poor; He hath sent me to heal the brokenhearted, to preach deliverance to the captives, and recovery of sight to the blind, to set at liberty them that are bruised, to preach the acceptable year of the Lord" (Luke 4:18–19)**. Human exploitation troubled Jesus, and therefore he chased the money changers out of the temple of God. **"And Jesus went into the Temple of God, and cast out all of them that sold and bought in the Temple, and overthrew the tables of the money changers, and the seats of them that sold doves, and said unto them, it is written, my House shall be called the House of Prayer; but ye have made it a den of thieves" (Matt. 21:12–16)**. This is Jesus' warning about money changers in the temple of God. Money is man's medium of exploitation. Judas betrayed Jesus for thirty pieces of silver. Money changers (exploiters) should not be in the temple of God; only individuals who desire to become children of God belong there. Jesus consistently emphasized that life was about *priorities* as expressed to three men who did not respond to the call: **"Come follow me, and I will make you fishers of men" (Matt. 4:18-22)**. Jesus is saying, "I will teach you how to save lives." A "certain" man said to Jesus he would follow him, but he said, "Lord, let me first go away and bury my father." Jesus said to him, **"Follow me, and let the dead bury the dead" (Matt. 8:22)**. This, indeed, was a hard statement. But Jesus was saying, "I know that you feel a sacred duty to ensure a decent burial for your deceased father. However, your father is dead, and there is nothing that you can do for him. Some undertaker who is physically alive but spiritually dead will dispose of the body, because your father's spirit is already before the throne of God. Tomorrow is not promised to you. There is nothing that the living can do for the dead and nothing that the dead can do for the living. Life *(living in the present moment)* is far more important than physical death."

In fact, Jesus was saying that the tragedy of life is that too often the non-embraced moment becomes a missed opportunity to do great things. Therefore, if you understand that the truth has come to you in the present moment, the decision as to what to do is up to you. "Come follow me, and I will make you fishers of men, teaching you how to save souls." Jesus was asking the man if he knew how to prioritize life. If so, "*Let the dead bury the dead.*" Of course, the man chose to go and bury his dead father. But there was another man who wanted to follow Jesus. **"'Lord, I will follow thee, but let me first go and bid them farewell, which are at my house.' And Jesus said unto him, 'No man having put his hand to the plow, and looking back, is fit for the Kingdom of God" (Luke 9:61–62).** The same demand and the same opportunity are extended to the second man. Through Jesus, individuals come to know the truth by acting. Every individual stands at the crossroads of decision (life). Life is about decision making. An individual can choose the broad way or the narrow way.

In every social interaction of life, an individual is confronted with choice(s)—and of course you cannot evade making decisions because life is dynamic; it does not stand still. Indeed, *time* marches on, because God is *Time*. God is alpha and omega, the beginning and the end. Thankfully God grants us a lifespan of *120* years (*based upon the length of time it took Noah to build the Ark)*, but because the wages of sin is death, most individuals can expect a *lifespan* of about seventy-five years. Moses spoke to the Israelites, saying, **"See, I have set before thee this day life and good, and death and evil...therefore choose life, that thou and thy seed may live" (Deut. 30:15–20)**. When Joshua was laying down the leadership of the Israelites, he presented them with the same choice: **"And if it seems evil unto you to serve the Lord, choose this day whom ye will serve" (Joshua 24:15)**. Jeremiah heard the voice of almighty God saying, **"Unto this people shalt thou say, thus said the Lord: Behold I have set before thee the way of life and the way of death" (Jeremiah 21:8).**

John Oxenham wrote in one of his poems:

To every man there openeth
A way and ways and a way
And the high soul treads the high way
And the low soul gropes the low;
And in between on the misty flats
The rests drift to and fro;
But to every man there openeth
A high way and a low;
And every man decideth
The way his soul shall go.

Without a doubt, Jesus confronted individuals with the truth, with a choice about which way they would go. Great living or low-life living has social consequences. There is never a "*free way.*" Life is never about looking backwards; it is about looking forward, because life is always in the making.

The third man wanted to know what he needed to do in order to inherit eternal life. **"Jesus said unto him, 'Go thy way, sell whatsoever thou hast, and give it to the poor, and thou shalt have treasure in heaven: And come, take up your cross and follow me.' And he was sad at this saying, and he went away grieved: For he had great possessions. And Jesus looked around about and said unto His disciples, how hardly they that have riches shall enter into the Kingdom of God; and the disciples were astonished at His words" (Mark 10:20–21).**

But Jesus answered again and said unto them, **"Children, how hard is it for them that trust in riches to enter into the Kingdom of God. It is easier for a camel to go through the eye of a needle, than for a rich man to enter into the Kingdom of God" (Mark 10:17–25).** For Jesus, the kingdom of God was on the inside of individuals, not on the outside. The kingdom of God is about righteousness, because God loves righteousness and hates sin. Life is about generous sharing, not selfish hoarding (Luke 12:13–21). Therefore, if a man places his trust in the material, visible world, then it is difficult for him to change his mind and decide to live spiritually. For if an individual's kingdom is on the inside, no one can break in and steal it; it can only be given away. **"Take heed, and beware of covetousness: For a man's life consisteth not in the abundance of the things which he possesseth" (Luke 12:15).**

Jesus is the *second Adam*. The first Adam brought sin into the world, because he yielded to the temptation of the devil through his disobedience to God's command—that is, not to eat of the tree of the *knowledge of good and evil* in the center of the Garden of Eden. Through one man's sin we all experience the ever-lurking presence of sin. **"Wherefore, as by one man sin entered into the world, and death by sin; and so death passed upon all men, for that all have sinned" (Romans 5:12).** Adam got us into sin, but Jesus gets us out of sin. **"For He hath made Him to be sin for us, who knew no sin, that we might be made the righteousness of God in Him" (2 Cor. 5:21).** The death referred to here is spiritual death, not physical death. Humankind was always physically born to physically die; only God does not die.

Sin is spiritual separation from God, because God hates sin and loves righteousness, but he loves us so much that he gave his only begotten Son, that whosoever believeth in him should not perish but have everlasting life (John 3:16). The first Adam yielded to the temptation of the devil to disobey God's command. Jesus, the second Adam, was tempted by the devil but never yielded. **"Then Jesus was led up by the Spirit into the wilderness to be tempted by the devil. And after He had fasted for forty days and nights, He then became hungry. And the tempter came and said to Him, 'If you are the son of God, command that these stones become bread.' But He answered and said, 'It is written, Man shall not live by bread alone, but by every word that proceeds out of the mouth of God'" (Matt. 4:1–11).** The devil tries to get Jesus to cast himself down, declaring that "you know that the angels will catch you." Jesus says to him, "On the other hand it is written, you shall not put God to the test." And again the devil takes Jesus to a very high mountain, and shows him all of the kingdoms of the world, and their glory, "and he said to Him, 'all these things I will give you, if you fall down and worship me.' Then Jesus said to him, 'Get behind me, Satan! For it is written, you shall worship the Lord God and serve Him only.'"

The devil tried to get Jesus to use his leadership power to serve himself, to have a self-serving life. Jesus told the devil that his *obligation* was to fulfill his religious *duty* to God, and therefore Jesus began to preach, saying, "Repent, for the Kingdom of heaven is at hand." Jesus, therefore, is God's beginning, God's in between, and God's end. But, most of all, Jesus is our measuring stick. The religion of Jesus is not for *double-minded pastors*; nor simple-minded individuals. **"Let this mind be in you, which was also in Christ Jesus" (Philippians 2:5).**

Finally, *men of the cloth*, Jesus is asking this question: Are you wearing the right clothes? The clothes of Jesus do not refer to outward appearance. They cannot be purchased at Saks Fifth Avenue, Neiman Marcus, or Macy's. Jesus' clothes do not have a designer label. We must put on the breastplate of righteousness and the helmet of soul salvation (Thessalonians 5:8; Ephesians 6:11–14). For it is certain that every individual has a spiritual appointment with a living God, and we should be careful about the clothes we wear. We cannot serve two masters. The question is, What do we think of Jesus? The clothes that we wear will define our answers. Jesus was born in a stable on the ground, wrapped in swaddling clothing with nowhere to lay his head, because there was no room in the *inn*. To be sure, it is difficult to find truth in high *corporate* places: motels, hotels, the Holiday Inn. Without a doubt, in God's kingdom, equal is equal, rather than equal being "more or less" equal.

PRAYER

God, we honor your holy name for the free will to live in hell physically and die and go to hell spiritually. Lord, thank you for the choice. We know that every tongue must confess and every knee must bow and acknowledge that Jesus is Lord, and in *him* you were reconciling the world unto *yourself*. Father God, help us to know that Jesus is *the* I Am before Abraham; Jesus is the Bread of Life; Jesus is the Light of the World; Jesus is the *Door* of the Sheep; Jesus is the Resurrection and the Life; Jesus is the True and Living Way; Jesus is the True Vine; Jesus is the Law and the Prophecy; and Jesus is the *Good Shepherd*. But most of all, Heavenly Father, let Jesus become the light that shines in me (and in all Christians). "But if we walk in the light, as He is in the light, we have fellowship one with another, and the blood of Jesus Christ His Son cleanses us from all sin" (1 John 1:7). Fix the *church*; fix the problem(s). God says, "Stop! Look! Listen! The church belongs to my only begotten Son, Jesus Christ; I can and I will fix the church." Amen!

CHAPTER FOUR

GOING TO CHURCH BEFORE YOU COME TO CHURCH

The church universal begins in the heart of an individual's mind with spiritual consciousness about consecrated sacredness; this is the invisible church. The family unit is the universal basis for *every society*. The first institution that God created was family. Although the church begins with sacred consecration in the mind towards heavenly things, it is then institutionalized in marriage in the home (we could call this "church in the family"). The family that prays together stays together. This is what going to church before coming to church is all about. In order to understand *praise* and *worship,* individuals must go to church become they come to church: They must bring sacredness and consecration to the church house, not go to the church house looking for sacredness. The entire book of

Genesis is an illumination of the consequences of the alienated relationship between God and human beings, which is the loss of sacredness. Of course, as humans we have an appetite for the profane. The stories of Adam and Eve, Cain and Abel, Noah and the Ark, and the Tower of Babel all symbolize the universal character of humankind's loss of sacredness and humankind's appetite for institutionalizing profaneness. The loss of sacredness occurred in the Garden of Eden with the disobedience of Adam and Eve.

In the Bible, God is the hero, not the prophets. In the twenty-first century, God is still the hero, not the pastors. God is not different. He is always the same—absoluteness. In the creation story God gives human beings free will; humans can choose to be faithful to God, or they can choose to serve their own ego interests. God is not a dictator of human will. Either way God gives human beings an exciting collective responsibility for this universe. God demands that we should be perfect in love. Individuals are perfect when they realize the purposes for which they were called into being: *Love God, and love your neighbor as you love yourself.* Therefore, individuals were created for sacred fellowship with God, not profaneness. God created goodness, and human beings created disobedience and sin. Pride is the basic element of the loss of sacredness by human beings. Sinning does not always come from a lack of knowledge. Adam and Eve understood God's command. Do not *"mess with the apples,"* or, do not attempt to play God.

Man is the *tree of life*, because he carries the seed of life. God's instruction to Adam and Eve about not eating of the tree of life (the knowledge of good and evil) was about human sexuality. Adam was the *tree* that God placed in the center of the Garden of Eden. From the top of an individual's head to his or her sexual anatomy and from the bottom of his or her feet to his or her sexual anatomy is, geometrically, the same distance in length. Thus at the center of every individual's body is their sexual anatomy. Without a doubt, a woman is and will always be the apple of a man's eye. The disobedience of Adam and Eve in the Garden of Eden was about lustful sexuality—sexuality without agape love. Adam and Eve did not cover their mouths because they had eaten an apple. They covered their sexual organs because they instinctively knew that they had violated God's divine command.

In other words, in all instances human beings always attempt to cover up that which commits or is in violation of moral order. The question is, *why*? Moreover, God did not make a lambskin to cover their mouths, but their sexual organs. When the spirit of God asked why they were hiding, they said because they were naked. They were physically naked from the beginning. What then caused nakedness in their minds? The answer to the question is participating in *lustful* sexuality without *agape love* towards each other. Making love is about moral obligation. God obligates himself to us first—that is, before he demands that we obligate ourselves to him. However, God is not a *divine Santa Claus;* he does not obligate himself to us and then willingly accept us serving the devil. This is why the first commandment is "thou shall not commit idolatry"—that is, thou shall have no other god before me.

A child then *ought to be* to be an expression of love (and moral obligation). The street concept is the "F" word for making love—that is, *erotic* sexual love. The "F" word is about human sexuality without *agape* love. In modern America, sexuality is highly correlated with the moral decay of our society: having sex without *agape,* or godly, love. Sex is purely an expression of *eros*. Hence, the loss of sacredness among human beings is directly related to the disobedience of Adam and Eve in the Garden of Eden.

The invisible church (in the individual's conscience, as described earlier) is morally broken, and therefore the church in the home is broken. This fact is reflected in the breakdown of family structure in American social life. Too many individuals go to the visible institutional church looking for meaning rather than bringing meaning to the visible institutional church. The spiritual void in their lives (holes in their souls) makes them easy prey for double-minded pastors. When I was growing-up there was a black and white western series on television called *Death Valley Days.* Today, in modern America, double-minded pastors with their prosperity-gospel message have helped to institute a "living color version" in both black and white neighborhoods. Death does not require conscious decision-making because individuals have no choice in physical death, since death is like unto a thief in the night; no individual knows the day or time (Matt. 24:36). Of course, if individuals had a choice in physical death, *most* individuals would choose to live forever.

Individuals need to be reminded that life is its own basis for meaning; death is not. The social meaning of death has ultimate significance for life on earth, not life somewhere else like "*heaven.*" Individuals die in a real world, not in an illusionary world. Death simply says, (a) God is a just God, because all individuals die and because death is universal in nature; (b) God is God, humans are humans, life is life, death is death—and more importantly, equal is equal, and therefore equal is not more or less equal. To be sure, God's judgment is the only reality. It is for this reason alone that suicide is a non-reality. Why commit suicide when all an individual needs is the patience to wait on God? For after all, physical death is inevitable, it is just a matter of time. All individuals know that they are going to physically die and of course most intelligent individuals do not want to know when they are going to die, they simply want the occasion to be a surprise; they want to simply go to sleep and slip into the big sleep, not waking up.

To live consciously, however, is to be involved in moral decision-making; moral decision-making is what helps us avoid spiritual death. Only human beings can understand morality, simply because we are conscious of our physical death. Lower forms of animal life are not conscious of physical death. If dogs were conscious of physical death they would not run after cars. But as humans we can understand morality simply because we are aware of physical death and of having a conscience. To act, then, is to be ethical because life is bound inexorably to moral choices. For after all, life requires conscious action because decisions have consequences; we choose our behavior, we choose our consequence. Rather than live as conscious beings, individuals glorify death (unconsciousness) as the *social* meaning of life. We do not know when we are going to die physically, and we do not want to know the time or day; only God knows the time, because it is appointed to die once and to receive judgment afterwards. God is the *Timekeeper*, because he is *Time*.

God's Vision for the Church

God's vision for the Christian church is vastly different from that of the corporate vision of double-minded pastors. God's church is not a building built by human hands. **"For every house is built by some man, but He that built all things is God" (Hebrews 3:4).** Ownership of the church is not "obtained" through record declaration with the IRS but is a part of God's divine order. The church was in the mind of God from the beginning: **"In the beginning God created the heaven and earth" (Genesis 1:1).** Therefore, **"If any man speak, let him speak as the oracles of God: If any man minster, let him do it as of the ability of which God giveth: That God in all things maybe glorified through Christ Jesus, to whom be praise and dominion forever and ever. Amen" (1 Peter 4:11).** The charge that God gives to every pastoral leader is simply this: **"I charge thee therefore before God, and the Lord Jesus Christ, who shall judge the quick and the dead at His appearing and His kingdom; preach the word; be instant in season, out of season; reprove, rebuke, exhort with all longsuffering and the doctrine. For the time will come when they will not endure sound doctrine, but after their own lusts shall they heap to themselves teachers, having itching ears: And they shall turn away their ears from the truth, and shall be turned unto fables" (2 Timothy 4:1–4).**

Corporate church greed is turning parishioners away from the truth because too many individuals are being driven outside of the church to psyche venues—*where there is no saving grace.* Of course, living by the flesh will cause an individual to do all sorts of *wicked* things. But we also know **"that in the dispensation of the fullness of times He might gather together in one all things in Christ, both which are in heaven, and which are on earth; even in Him" (Ephesians 1:10).** For God has allowed all things to be placed under the authority of Jesus who is sitting at the right hand of the Father preparing a place for us, being our intercessor unto the Father. Because "all" individuals must come through the Son in order to get to the Father; "Because every tongue must confess and every knee must bow and confess that Jesus is the Christ, the Son of the living God." **"And hath put all things under His feet, and gave Him to be the head over all things to the Church, which is His body, the fullness of Him that filleth all in all" (Ephesians 1:22–23).**

Of course, the Bible says, **"For a workman is worthy of his meat" (Matt. 10:10).** Therefore, no one should deny pastoral leadership the ability to provide for themselves as well as their families. However, **"all things must be done decently and in order" (1 Corinthians 14:40).** For after all, **"God is not the author of confusion, but of peace, as in all churches of the saints" (1 Corinthians 14:33).** The question is, Why is there so much confusion in modern-day mega-churches, as well as other churches in general? Is the answer money? Too much money for some churches, and too little for other churches. Of course, what is lost in the shuffle is sound doctrine regarding salvation and being born again.

God established a *divine order* for the church in order that we might be able to live by the fruits of the Spirit, not the vanity of the flesh. **"But the fruit of the Spirit is love, joy, peace, longsuffering, gentleness, goodness, faith, meekness, temperance: Against such there is no law" (Galatians 5:22–23). "Therefore being justified by faith, we have peace with God through our Lord Jesus Christ" (Romans 5:1).** Justification is by *faith* through Jesus Christ, whether individuals give money or don't give money, justification is not by pastoral leadership.

Peter reminds us precisely what salvation and being born again is all about as it relates to the ***"seven graces" and "climbing Jacobs' ladder to Heaven"*** **(Genesis 28:10–15).** God created individuals to do *his will and consequently to give him the glory, honor, and praise*, and his will is that we love and serve him and conversely that we love and serve each other. **"Thou shalt not bow down thyself to them, nor serve them: For I the Lord thy God am a jealous God, visiting the iniquity of the fathers upon the children unto the third and fourth generation of them that hate me" (Exodus 20:5).**

The church is one of the *two central* institutions in God's dispensation (*divine ordering of things*), and the other is the family, since the only institutions God created were family and church, and in that order. However, it is possible to theologically argue that God created the church first because the Garden of Eden symbolically was Adam's and Eve's church. God had continued to dress and keep it by being obedient to

God's will. Peter says, **"Grace and peace be multiplied unto you through the knowledge of God, and of Jesus our Lord. According as His divine power hath given unto us all things that pertain unto life and godliness, through the knowledge of Him that hath called us to glory and virtue: Whereby are given unto us exceeding great and precious promises: That by these ye might be partakers of the divine nature, having escaped the corruption that is in the world through lust. And beside this, giving all diligence, add to your faith virtue; and to virtue knowledge; and to knowledge, temperance; and to temperance patience; and to patience godliness; and to godliness brotherly kindness; and to brotherly kindness charity. For if these things be in you, and abound, ye shall neither be barren nor unfruitful in the knowledge of our Lord Jesus Christ. But he that lacketh these things is blind, and cannot see afar off, and hath forgotten that he was purged from his old sins. Wherefore the rather, brethren, give diligence to make your calling and election sure: For if ye do these things, ye shall never fall: For so an entrance shall be ministered unto you abundantly into the everlasting Kingdom of our Lord and savior Jesus Christ" (2 Peter 1:2–11).**

I am reminded of the story of King Hezekiah of Judah, who was upright in the sight of the Lord. Hezekiah ushered in civil and religious reforms, had a powerful personal relationship with God, and most of all had a powerful prayer life. But Hezekiah had a serious weakness: he showed little interest or wisdom in *visionary planning* for the future and spiritual protection for others, as well as for the spiritual heritage that he had enjoyed from his forefathers, even though he had a close personal relationship with God, like that of his father King David. However, he opulently displayed his wealth to the messengers from Babylon, creating a political/military problem. To be sure, God *reminded* Hezekiah, "Get your house in order; *you are going to die.*" Double-minded pastors should remember that God's message is still the same: "You are going to die, and after death—judgment." No one is exempt from the valley of the shadow of death walk.

Churches are places where God's saints meet and for those who desire to become saints in order to praise and worship God. **"For the wrath of God is revealed from heaven against all ungodliness of men, who hold the truth in unrighteousness; because that which may be known of God is manifest in them; for God has shewed it unto them. For the invisible things of Him from the creation of the world are clearly seen, being understood by the things that are made, even His eternal power and godhead; so that they are without excuse because that, when they knew God, they glorified Him not as God, neither were thankful, but became vain in their imaginations, and their foolish heart was darkened. Professing themselves to be wise, they became fools" (Romans 1:18–22)**. God's purpose for the church is spiritual unity and moral integration, not cultural confusion and separatism. Finally, my Christian friends, *all churches* have *temporal/transitory,* legitimate ministerial payroll notes, mortgage notes, utilities notes, and so on. But, we should never forget that all individuals—be they clergy or laity—have a *soul* note that must be paid eternally.

PRAYER

God, we earnestly pray that *every* family come into revelatory knowledge of the meaning of your *Son's* death, the shedding of *his* precious blood, *his* resurrection, and *his* ascension with all power in *his* hands through *faith,* in order that we might be able to receive soul salvation and be born again of the Spirit of God. For without *faith* it is impossible to please God. *Faith* comes by hearing and hearing by the Word of God. Fix the *church*; fix the problem(s). God says, "Stop! Look! Listen! The church belongs to my only begotten Son, Jesus Christ; I can and I will fix the church." Amen!

CHAPTER FIVE

SHARING THE LOVE OF GOD

How do we share the love of God that was represented in the life of Jesus?

If we go to church before we come to church, invariably we will understand the spiritual meaning of individual as well as corporate *worship*. Worship is for God. Praise is for us (churchgoers). The invisible church has lost its moral power, and as a consequence, the visible church has lost the moral power to speak the truth in love. The invisible church is about moral conscience: speaking the truth in love and/or speaking truth to power. Consequently, the institutional church has become focused on building itself into a corporate empire through individualistic economic processes. This is why in many communities, especially urban communities, there is a church building on every street corner. This social fact indicates an institutional leadership problem. The institutional church has lost its moral power for four main reasons:

First of all, we have forgotten the *promise of God.* God has promised to never leave us alone, and, of course, if we are faithful, God will supply our needs (Philippians 4:19; Deut. 8:18). **"And my God shall supply all your needs according to His riches in glory in Christ Jesus" (Philippians 4:19). "But you shall remember the Lord thy God, for it is He who is giving you power to make wealth, that He may confirm His covenant which He swore to you and your fathers, as it is this day" (Deut. 8:18). "But I shall establish my covenant with you and you shall enter the ark—you and your sons and your wife, and your sons' wives with you" (Genesis 6:18).** The "*covenant*" is about God unconditionally obligating himself to us, universal humankind.

Second, we have forgotten the *principles of God.* It, indeed, is unfortunate that even churchgoers have forgotten the principles of God: Love God with all your heart, soul, and might. Shun wickedness; seek God and his righteousness, and all these things shall be added unto you. Do unto others as you would have them do unto you. Love people and use things. Do not love things and use people. Many individuals have the principles backwards. Indeed, money is a cruel master.

Third, the church is not fulfilling the *Great Commission.* The church, in order to become the church, must be willing to leave its physical premises in order to attend to the *promise of God* and effectively fulfill the *Great Commission* **(Matt. 28:18–20): "All authority has been given to *Me* in heaven and on earth. Go, therefore, and make disciples of all nations, baptizing them in**

the name of the Father and the Son and the Holy Spirit and teaching them to observe all that I have commanded you; and lo, I am with thee always, even unto the end of the age." In other words, God has promised to be with us through the good times and the bad (*all of our days*). Unfortunately, institutional churches have turned inward to serve their own ego interests and the ego interests of double-minded pastors, rather than serving the needs of the communities in which they exist. Unfortunately, double-minded pastors want to be glorified, rather than sanctified, rectified, and above all justified by their faith in God.

The orientation of institutional churches is towards building a materialistic empire rather than empowering individuals from the inside out to live creative religious lives. To be sure, Jesus empowered individuals from the inside to the outside, not vice versa; take, for example, the man at the pool of Bethesda story in John 5:1–17. There was a feast of the Jews, and Jesus goes to Jerusalem to attend. Jesus encounters a man at the sheep's gate pool. At this pool lay many who were ill, waiting for the angel of the Lord to come down and move the waters. But this certain man who had been there for thirty-eight years gets the attention of Jesus. Jesus knew that the man had been there for a long time. Therefore, Jesus says to the man, "*Do you wish to get well?*" The sick man answers him, "Sir, I have no man to put me in the pool when the water is stirred up, but while I am coming another steps in front of me." Jesus says to him, "*Arise, take up your pallet, and walk.*" And immediately the man becomes well, and takes up his pallet and begins to walk. I can imagine that the conversation between Jesus and the lame man went something like this: Sir, the *kingdom of God (internal power)* is within each individual, not on the outside—externally—in a pool or otherwise. In other words, the power to transform "your*self*" lies within you, not outside of you; it is called the *power within*. The kingdom of God is already at hand, repent; change the inner man. People do not save people, otherwise you would not have been in the same condition for thirty-eight years. I am not going to place you in the pool either; however, I will *help* you release the *power of God* that is within you in order that you might be healed from your affliction. I will not enslave myself to you because I must be about *my father's business*: Get up, pick up your pallet, and walk in the *Spirit*, because it is mind over matter. Therefore, free your *mind* in order that your *behind* might follow. Of course, the hypocrites (scribes, Pharisees, and Sadducees) who could have helped the lame man were the most critical; people do not save people: **"Who made you well and told you to take up your pallet and walk? Don't you know that it is the Sabbath? Who is this man that said to you take up your pallet and walk on the Sabbath?" (John 5:11–12)**. Of course, Jesus' answer to these questions is recorded in **Mark 2:27–28: "The Sabbath was made for man, and not man for the Sabbath. Consequently, the Son of Man is Lord even of the Sabbath."**

Fourth, and finally, the institutional church has lost its moral power to speak the *truth* in *love*. The question is, why? Most of us are familiar with the Mount of Transfiguration story, featuring Peter, James, and John, in Luke 9:28–40. Jesus takes his trusted disciples to the mountainside to pray. While Jesus is praying, the appearance of his face changes, his clothing becomes white and gleaming, and he is talking to Moses and Elijah. The disciples are sleeping, and when they awaken, they see Jesus talking to Moses and Elijah. Peter says, "Master, it is good for us to be here; let us make three tabernacles: one for you, one for Moses, and one for Elijah." Instantly, a cloud forms and overshadows them, and a voice comes out of the cloud, saying: "*This is My Son, My Chosen One; listen to Him.*"

The original disciples, just like the double-minded pastors of the twenty-first century, desired to build physical temples (sacred tents). The next day, Jesus and the three disciples came down from the mountainside, and they were met by a great multitude. One man shouted out, "Great Teacher, I beg you to heal my son, for he is my only boy. I begged your disciples to cast out the demons, but they could not." Jesus healed the man's son and demonstrated to the disciples that they had power and did not know what to do with it. This is the plight of contemporary double-minded pastors; they indeed have power but do not know what to do with it.

The response that Jesus gave two thousand years ago is appropriate even more so today: **"O unbelieving and perverted generation, how long shall I be with you and put up with you?" (Luke 9:41)**. Just like the original disciples, the church has lost its moral power or authority; the church has power but does not know what to do with it, because God says he will give us pastors after our own hearts (double-minded men). If we want double-minded pastors, we will have double-minded pastors.

To be sure, Jesus is coming back for a church without a spot or wrinkle, and rest assured, it will not be the institutional, visible church. Many churches appear to be focused on heaven but have a big, old backdoor to the world. But wherever the spirit of God is present, love will work miracles. When we have a church where love works miracles, we can outrun the devil (or *evil*). Elijah outran evil, and so can we, because Jesus declared, "These things that I do, greater things shall you do." Job outlasted the afflictions of the devil and declared, **"All of my days I shall wait upon the Lord" (Job 1–5).** God allowed the devil to test Job. Job loses his *wealth and health, and he laments even the day he was born.* However, in the final analysis, Job outlasted the afflictions of the devil. **"For affliction does not come from the dust, neither does trouble sprout from the ground, for man is born for trouble, as sparks fly upward. But as for me, I would seek God, and I would place my cause before God" (Job 5:6–8).** God is spirit, and they who worship *him* must worship *him* in spirit and in truth. God is just, and his mercy endures forever.

PRAYER

Father in heaven, we bless your name. We know that you love us so much that you gave your only *begotten Son,* that whosoever believeth in *you* shall not perish but have eternal life. Make us ever so mindful that life is not found in the abundance of things, but in love and service to others. Above all, help us to remember that money will always come when we are doing the right thing. For King David declared that he has never seen the righteous go hungry or the seed of the righteous beg for bread. In the priceless name of Jesus we pray: Fix the *church*; fix the problem(s). God says, "Stop! Look! Listen! The church belongs to my only begotten Son, Jesus Christ; I can and I will fix the church." Amen!

CHAPTER SIX

REPAIRING LIVES TO BECOME CREATIVELY MORE RELIGIOUS

Visible, institutional churches should function as *spiritual hospitals* for both saved as well as unsaved sinners. The church universal must find creative ways to repair individual and family-related brokenness. Churches must be made up of spiritually-minded individuals, because spiritually-minded individuals create unity and harmony, not discord and quarreling. Double-minded pastors are replicating materialists rather than replicating spiritualists. The New Testament writer Paul raises the question in 1 Corinthians 3:9–11: What kind of church do you want? One that is made up of spiritually minded individuals? Or one that is made up of unspiritually minded individuals? Paul was making the point that the Corinthian church was being defiled by some, because they were quarreling, misbehaving, grumbling, and being divisive; therefore, they were in danger of receiving the severest punishment.

In other words, to split a church is one of the worst sins, because the church is the institutional representation of the temple of God; it is holy. Therefore, in verse 11, Paul reminds us that no individual can lay a foundation other than the one that is laid, which is Jesus Christ. The rock upon which the church was built was not Peter, but *Christ/the Righteous One,* because Christ is not a person or a proper name. Christ is a title meaning *righteousness* or *the Righteous One*. Therefore, to Paul it is unreasonable to argue about who is the *top dog* in the church. We are fellow workers with God. We are God's field. The church's one true foundation is the righteousness of Jesus Christ, the Righteous One. Therefore, church unity must be based upon the eternal righteousness of Jesus. In order to make his point, Paul refers to the church three dimensionally: (1) the church as individual Christian believers, (2) the church as God's field—the collective body of believers, and (3) the church as a visible institution. The church is both invisible and visible.

The invisible church begins in the heart of an individual's mind with consciousness concerning the reality of God, which in turn is consecration towards righteousness. Hence, the invisible Church is consummated in marriage—the family. Therefore, the invisible church is made manifest as the church in the home. The institutional church is broken primarily because of family brokenness. The question is: How does the church repair family brokenness? Nowhere in all of Christianity is the social fact of family brokenness more vivid than in the *black church community*, the community in which the church primarily is made up of the elderly, women, and children. The stark, *glaring* absence of the physical presence of black men in churches is indicative of an institutional leadership problem. To be sure, it is *biblically prophetic* that men build churches and women attend churches. Without a doubt, in the black church the pastor is the only *rooster* in the henhouse.

The best example of who builds God's spiritual church is the story of Jesus' encounter with the woman at *Jacob's well* in John 4:7–30. To paraphrase the Scriptures, Jesus encounters a beautiful Samaritan woman at Jacob's well. *He* asked the woman to give him a drink of water. The Samaritan woman replied in indignation, "How is it that you, being a Jew, ask me, being a Samaritan woman, for a drink of water?" (For Jews have no dealings with Samaritans). Jesus answered and said to her: "If you knew the *gift of God*, and who it is that says to you, 'Give Me a drink,' you would have asked Him and He would have given you living water." The woman declared, "You do not have anything to even get some water. You are not greater than Jacob our father." Jesus answered, "Everyone that drinks of this water shall thirst again, but whosoever drinks of the water that I shall give him shall never thirst; but the water that I shall give him shall become in him a well of water springing up to eternal life." The woman replied, "Sir, give me this water." Jesus said, "Go, call thy husband, and come hither." The woman replied, "I have no husband." Jesus said to her, "You have well said, 'I have no husband,' for you have had five husbands and the husband you have now is not yours; this you have truly said." The woman said, "I perceive that you are a prophet." Jesus replied to the woman, "God is a Spirit, and those that worship Him, must worship in spirit and truth." So the woman left her water pots and ran into the city, saying, "Come see a *real man* who told me all the things I have done."

Double-minded pastors do not want *real men* in the church. It is obvious even to the casual observer why double-minded pastors in the black community do not want the physical presence nor the leadership influence of *strong black men* in the church. It is about *ego and being* the only *rooster* in the henhouse. Even to the casual observer, the reason is obvious: It is far more difficult for a man to hustle (*pimp*) another man out of his labor (*money*) than it is for a man to *pimp* a woman out of her labor (*money*) or even her husband's labor. To be sure, without the presence of strong spiritually minded men involved in the communal life of the institutional church, the church cannot heal its institutional brokenness or that of families. Black double-minded pastors are dealing with leadership money separation rather than moral spiritual integration. Consequently, black double-minded ministers are playing on the emotions of women, since women primarily make up black church congregations, rather than teaching and exemplifying love and service. In **Matthew 22:37** and in **Mark 12:29–31**, Jesus was asked, **"Master, which is the great commandment in the Law?"** Jesus said unto him, **"Thou shalt love the Lord thy God with all thy heart, and with all thy soul, and with thy entire mind. This is the first and great commandment, and the second is like unto it, Thou shalt love thy neighbor as thyself."**

On these two commandments hang all the law and the prophets. Therefore, the visible institutional church has two functions: *worship* and *service*. Worship is about praising God for all of his goodness and mercy, not just material wealth or prosperity. Worship is for God. Praise is for individuals. The gospel of prosperity that is preached by double-minded pastors transforms churches into individualistic economic processes, rather than community-based developmental institutions. Churches ought to be institutions that build institutions, starting with building strong family units—not physical, individualistic monuments of self-glorification.

PRAYER

Lord, hear our prayer, for the just shall live by faith; not sight. Faith comes by hearing and hearing by the Word of God. We pray that every family household is a praying home and that every church house is a house of prayer— not a den of thieves, but that Christians take care of the poor, the elderly, the widows, and the orphans. In Jesus' name we pray: Fix the *church*; fix the problem(s). God says, "Stop! Look! Listen! The church belongs to my only begotten Son, Jesus Christ; I can and I will fix the church." Amen!

CHAPTER SEVEN

THE GOSPEL OF PROSPERITY BY DOUBLE-MINDED PASTORS

Too often, religion in the modern era is corporate-secular and circuslike, oriented toward entertainment (staged productions) rather than toward spiritual enlightenment. In other words, it is a scheme of religious beliefs about *prosperity* that is intellectually somewhat sophisticated but doomed to failure because it is based on lies rather than *biblical truths*. History is made mostly by irresponsible leaders. This fact alone is a social testament to the underdeveloped spiritual character of the human mind. Mental immaturity (spiritual malnutrition of the brain) comes from individuals acting in dehumanizing ways towards themselves and others. Biological maturation (age) is not an insurance policy against juvenile delinquency or mental immaturity. God gives Christianity to individuals to free us from the spiritual price tag on sin, but the money changers (and *takers*) of this world have abused its powers as a ways and means to exploit and enslave. Few want freedom; most want to learn how to be happy slaves. Without a doubt, freedom is not free; it requires individual and collective responsibility, credibility, and accountability. It is for this reason alone, with many exchanging freedom for enslavement, that institutional Christianity has become the most successful form of *tax-free* vulgar capitalism in the twenty-first century. Of course, there are too many *corporate, double-minded mega-church* examples to even begin to call the roll.

Likewise, governmental political ideologies are simply ways to disguise privileges for the few; they have become a fairly sophisticated way of circumventing the concept of social cost accountability. Both governing political ideologies, as well as corporate Christianity, exclude the truth about human life. All of humankind is equal in dignity before the throne of God, because death is the social equalizer, and after physical death comes God's spiritual judgment: ***"And inasmuch as it is appointed for men to die once and after this comes judgment"*** **(Hebrews 9:27)**. Since the wages of sin is death, God does not judge us for our sins; *God's spiritual judgment* is about the good left undone. Of course, if God judged us for our sins, we would all be *sleeping* in our graves.

Modern societies can no longer remain half free and half slave. The life of Abraham Lincoln is a stark reminder of this fact.

The world community must become oriented towards collective stewardship and a new world order (moral order) that is not dominated by institutional cultural racism, classism, sexism, militarism, negativism, and economic exploitation. The ideas for such a world order are inculcated in the Christian tradition, but must be resurrected through a reaffirmation of the *theology* and *religion* of Jesus and an abandonment of the theology and corporate religion about Jesus.

To be sure, *double-minded pastors* have deliberately *distorted* and *hijacked* the teachings of Jesus for personal economic gain. The mind of God is universal in nature and cannot be held captive, even through historic *canonization*. Christianity is an affirmation in action of the *will of God*, which is that we love one another. On the one hand, corporate Christianity unwittingly espouses that money is *god*, and of course the membership motto is "*come as you are, stay as you are,* but leave your money behind." On the other hand, spiritually authentic Christianity is about repentance, *divine* forgiveness of sins, cross bearing (responsibility and accountability), faith in God rather than faith in the things of this world (*idolatry*)—and of course, we can come as we are, but we must repent, be baptized, become born of the *Spirit of God,* and change our way of living. For broad is the way that leads to destruction, and narrow is the *gate* that leads to eternal life for the soul. **"Enter by the narrow gate; for the gate is wide, and the way is broad that leads to destruction, and many are those who enter by it. For the gate is small, and the way is narrow that leads to life, and few are those who find it. Beware of the false prophets, who come to**

you in sheep's clothing, but inwardly are ravenous wolves" (Matt. 7:13–15). Jesus commanded *pastoral leaders* to feed the sheep as his undershepherds, not to become *double-minded men* who eat the sheep.

In order to hear we must listen. If we listen we can learn. We listen to learn and learn to listen. If we learn of God, we will know how to live, not how to die. God is the God of the living, not the dead. The devil is the *spiritual power* that wants an individual dead both spiritually and physically. However, the eternal question is, How do we (*I*) live? But, more importantly, what are we willing to sacrifice in order to live the way we say we want to live?

Unfortunately, in the twenty-first century Christian church, there are too many double-minded pastors in pulpits across the nation cooking up false spiritual formulas for personal gain and fame. These double-minded pastors have individuals chasing after prosperity clouds with no water in them, and of course no one is experiencing economic prosperity but the double-minded pastors themselves. When God asked individuals to follow after a cloud in Exodus 13:21–22, everything that the individuals needed was in the cloud: physical light (fire) was in the cloud, so the people could see by night; water was in the cloud; and manna (food from heaven) was in the cloud. Double-minded pastors need to repent while there is still time, because it is clear that they are not on *God's spiritual payroll.* God is not pleased with the spiritual prostitution that is prevalent in the corporate church. The church is the bride of Jesus, and he is coming back for a church without a spot or wrinkle, and rest assured, it will not be the visible corporate church.

Traditionally, black people understood that material prosperity evolved through getting a "*quality education*" and "fighting against injustice" (as in the civil rights movement). In the modern era, prosperity has become hero worship (living vicariously through others). Real prosperity comes through obedience to the *will of God* as expressed in the *Word of God.* The fruits of the Spirit are Jesus' measurement of prosperity: **"But the fruit of the Spirit is love, joy, peace, patience, kindness, goodness, faithfulness, gentleness, self-control; against such things there is no law. Now those who belong to Christ Jesus have crucified the flesh with its passions and desires. If we live by the Spirit, let us also walk by the Spirit. Let us not become boastful, challenging one another, envying one another" (Galatians 5:22–26). "We should bear one another's burdens and thus fulfill the law of Christ. For if anyone thinks he is something when he is nothing, he deceives himself" (Galatians 6:1–3).**

The will of God is not complex but simple in nature: **"Love one another as I have loved you." "For God so loved the world that He gave His only begotten Son, that whosoever believeth in Him should not perish, but have everlasting life" (John 3:16).** To be sure, Jesus took the Ten Commandments that were given to Moses and reduced them to the *two great commandments:* Love God with all your heart, soul, and might—do not commit idolatry; and love your neighbor as you love yourself—do unto others as you would have them do to you. The gospel of good news that Jesus taught is based primarily upon *redemptive* *suffering*, not material prosperity. Indeed, material prosperity is not primary in the gospel of Jesus. For Jesus, prosperity is about the "fruits of the *Spirit,"* eternal salvation for the soul. Therefore, for Jesus *redemptive suffering* for the sake of *righteousness* is the key to spiritual prosperity. Jesus said that he was born into the world for this cause, and of course someone said, "What cause?" Jesus replied, "To suffer in order that God might have someone to bear witness to the truth." When Peter and John were going to the temple for prayer, they encountered a "lame beggar." Just as they were about to enter the temple, the beggar asked for alms. Peter and John said, "Look at us," and then Peter said, **"I do not possess silver and gold, but what I do have I give to you: In the name of Jesus Christ the Nazarene—walk" (Acts 3:1–10).** The beggar's feet and ankles were strengthened, and he leaped up; he stood upright and began to walk, and he entered the temple with Peter and John, walking, leaping, and praising God. Prosperity for the beggar became healing, not silver or gold.

The motivation for attending church should not be financial prosperity, but spiritual development and family restoration. Likewise, the motivation for preaching should not be obtaining money or personal gain. Obviously, an individual should not tithe in order to get more money. Tithing ought to be an outward expression of an inward spiritual reality. God is not a divine *Santa Claus.* God does not bestow blessings upon individuals and expect nothing in return. In short, God is not a *fool* nor is he *fooled*; God is not going to serve individuals and then have individuals serve the devil. **"As snow in summer, and as rain in harvest, so honor is not seemly for a fool... A whip for the horse,**

a bridle for the ass, and a rod for a fool's back. . . Answer not a fool according to his folly, lest he be wise in his own conceit. He that sends a message by the hand of a fool cuts off the feet, and drinks damage" (Proverbs 26:1–6). The cult leader Jim Jones instituted a Kool-Aid drinking cult. Modern-day, double-minded pastors have instituted prosperity cults, and of course, more disturbing is the fact that the prerequisite for membership is the willingness to reveal one's personal income tax returns.

In the first century, Jesus chased the money changers out of the temple **(Matt 21:12–13)**. Jesus entered the temple and overturned the tables of the money changers and said, **"It is written, *my* house shall be called a house of prayer, but you are making it a robbers' den."** Prayer is internal introspection. This is why in **Matthew 6:6** it says, **"But thou, when thou prayest, enter into thy closet, and when thou has shut the door, pray to thy Father which is in secret; and thy Father which seeth in secret shall reward thee openly."** In other words, when we pray we should go into the closet of our own mind, shutting out the chatter of the world, and bringing the *I, the EGO,* under submission to the *me, the God-force* in us. The *me* is the spiritual dimension in every individual that says, "Lord, have mercy upon me, a sinner and a wretch undone."

In the twenty-first century they (the *robbers—or* double-minded pastors) are back stronger than ever, alive and doing well. These double-minded pastors were "called" supposedly to feed the sheep, but too many are eating the sheep. Jesus has said that he shall return for a church without a spot or wrinkle. Double-minded pastors are singing, "Pass me by *gentle Savior,* because I am *certainly* not singing the Lord's song in a strange and foreign land; I am singing the world's money song (and am *money-hungry*)." In Houston I know one double-minded pastor who stood boldly and told the church congregation that God did not call him to preach. He chose preaching for the money and that the church was not paying him enough. The congregation was *sane-minded* enough; it did not have *malnutrition* of the brain and it *"[ran] the double-minded individual away."*

The church universal must become authentically more effective in order to embrace the concept of the community beyond the community, the church beyond the church, and above all the church without walls—a church not built by human hands. Too often, churches have turned inward to serve their own institutional egos. This fact expresses itself most profoundly in the decline of *moral servanthood* among pastoral leaders. To be sure, too many religious leaders have lost the sense of moral servanthood; rather than serving, they want to be served. Therefore, the twenty-first century church has ceased to be prophetic and has become pathetic. In order to be an effective pastoral leader, pastors must think in spiritual terms—but the church is an organization, and of course organizations must act politically without embracing partisan politics. These double-minded pastors have contributed immensely to the brainwashing of many individuals, robbing themselves of spiritual principles and moral values. In fact, double-minded pastors have helped to perpetuate *cultural Christianity* rather than *Christ-centered Christianity.* Authentic Christianity can never accommodate itself to secular culture. Daniel being placed in the lion's den by

King Darius must be Christianity's everlasting authentic example of nonaccommodation to secular, cultural idolatry (Daniel 6). It is time for the church to develop institutional strategies for initiating a *prophetic church reformation.*

The Christian church universal—especially *church leadership*—must become an example of moral character to the world, instead of the church being able to produce an exhibit of whatever sin is named. Double-minded pastors have enslaved the church to a vulgar form of *individualistic capitalism*, thereby rendering the institutional church virtually morally bankrupt. What kind of church do we want? I simply want to remind double-minded pastors of the New Testament writer Paul's exhortation in **1 Corinthians 3:9–11: "For we are God's fellow workers, you are God's field, God's building. According to the grace of God which was given to me, as a wise master builder I laid a foundation, and another is building upon it. But let each man be careful how he builds upon it. No man can lay a foundation other than the one which is laid, which is *Jesus Christ*."** In this passage of scripture, Paul raises the question: What kind of church do we want? Do we want a church that is made up of spiritually minded individuals, or one that is made up of unspiritually minded, secular individuals? In other words, *"do we want a church where love works miracles?"* Therefore, in verse 11 Paul reminds us that no individual can lay a foundation other than the one that is laid, which is Jesus Christ. The Christian church is Jesus: Jesus is the church.

The rock that the church was built upon was not Peter, but Christ-centered righteousness and Peter's *faith*, because Christ is not a person or proper name, it is a title that means *righteousness* or *the Righteous One*. The church's one true foundation is Christ-righteousness. The righteousness of Jesus is the *eternal* foundation of the church. In order to make his point, Paul refers to the church in three ways: the church as the individual Christian believer, the church as God's field—the collective body of believers, and the church as an institution. The church is both invisible and visible. The invisible church begins in the heart of an individual's mind and is consecrated towards righteousness (sacredness). That is, let the mind that was in Jesus Christ also be in you, because God is Universal Mind. The visible church is consummated in marriage—the family—that is, the church in the home. Christianity is a family faith, just like Judaism is a family faith. Every individual must find for himself or herself the baby in a manager in Bethlehem and follow that star to Jerusalem, and stand at the foot of the cross and hear someone sing: "Must Jesus bear the cross alone and all the world go free? No, there is a cross for everyone. There is a cross for me." Christmas is bigger than *gifts*. Blessed is he, heavenly Father, who knows how big Christmas is: For he who takes the gifts of Christmas must be willing to take the cross, and drink of Jesus' bitter cup.

Double-minded pastoral leaders do not want to drink of the bitter cup; they want the honeycomb. Which is why so many church homes on so many street corners do not know how to be what they are for others; they do not know how to serve the communities in which they exist. The visible church has two functions: worship and service. Worship is spiritual in nature and, as stated previously, is for God. Praise, as stated previously, is for individuals. Service is about the "church beyond the church" and the "community beyond the community," which includes the *Great Commission (Matt. 28:16–20)*. We should feed the hungry, clothe the naked, and provide for the widows and orphans. Jesus was asked, "When did we see you hungry and did not feed you, sick and did not visit you, and in prison and did not visit you?" Jesus replied: "*In as much as you have done it unto the least of them my brethren you have done it unto me.*"

Double-minded pastors have forgotten about the important principle of servant leadership; they simply go along in order to get along, in order to obtain money. Our greatest need as individuals, however, is for love, not money. When you love something that cannot love you in return, it can be said that you are a *fool*. Money can be a dangerous commodity, especially when individuals develop an inappropriate attitude towards it. **"No man can serve two masters: For either he will hate one, and love the other. You cannot serve God and money" (Matthew 6:24)**. Money is value neutral, neither good nor evil; it is simply a medium of exchange for goods and services. Our federal governmental system recognizes this fact, which is why our money is inscribed with "*In God We Trust.*" But secularists want to remove the slogan from United States' currency, and we know why: without recognition of God, money becomes the *God force, subverting the spiritual God of our forefathers*. Of course, many parents have failed to teach their children money-management skills, not to mention self-management skills.

Many Americans use money to create self-enslavement (dependency) rather than economic independence. When we fall prey to the temptations that money brings, we edge God out of our lives, and of course we cannot get enough. We need more money, want more money, and ultimately have to have more money. **"Consider your ways. You have sown much, and bring in little, you eat but you do not have enough, you drink but you are not filled, you wear clothes but you are not warm, you place your wages in a bag with a hole in it" (Haggai 1:3–6)**. All of us should be mindful of the fact that we might have house notes, car notes, or clothing notes, but God says that churches and individuals have soul notes that relate directly to the *Great Commission.* In **Matt. 28:18–20**, Jesus spoke to them: **"All authority has been given to me in heaven and on earth. Go therefore and make disciples of all nations, baptizing them in the name of the Father, and the Son, and the Holy Spirit, teaching them to observe all that I commanded you; and lo, I am with you always, even to the end of the age."**

In other words, the church ceases to be the church when it turns inward to serve both its own institutional ego interests as well as those of double-minded pastors. Jesus could have compromised his message to culturally accommodate the scribes, Pharisees, and Sadducees of his times. Instead, unlike double-minded pastors, Jesus chased the money changers out of the temple. To the dismay of many, the corporate prosperity gospel of popular religion has no "blood in it, no redemption in it, and no cross in it." In fact, one popular mega-corporate church has no *cross* visibly displayed on the corporate premises. Instead,

God is portrayed as a divine Santa Claus, inviting us to come and get our blessings (gifts). In short, come as you are and stay as you are—just leave your money at the door. Physical church growth does not glorify God, but double-minded pastors.

Indeed, money is a cruel master. Churches are dying spiritually and our culture is in moral decline; as a result, American society is becoming institutionally decadent, selfish, self-centered, and self-indulgent; it is characterized by the *me*, *myself*, and *I* syndrome—what is commonly called the personal pronoun disease. To be sure, God has spoken to his people in every generation, and his theological principles do not change from one generation to the next. We need to guard against allowing money to cause us to wander and drift away from the reality of God. Money cannot prevent an individual from experiencing the *"walk through the valley of the shadow of death."* Without a doubt, I have never seen a *U-Haul* following a hearse to the graveyard.

If you want to have a significant life, then look for opportunities to make a difference and above all creatively embrace the reality of God. If individuals simply desire to be successful in life (accumulating material possessions), then they turn inward to serve their own ego interests. *Significance* in life is about spiritualism and love and service to others. You came into the world with nothing, and your relatives are not going to allow you to take anything out, even if you have it written in an iron-clad will that you are to be buried with all of your earthly goods. Trust me: Your relatives will not honor your request. **"Take heed, and beware of greed: For man's life consists not**

in the abundance of things, which he possesses" (Luke 12:15). Therefore, aspire to inspire before you expire.

We need to guard against money choking off the *Word of God* in our lives. **"Guard yourself against the deceitfulness of riches, and the lust of other things entering in to choke off the *Word of God* and you become unfruitful" (Mark 4:19).** Love of money leads people to forget themselves. Even Clint Eastwood declared that for a fistful of dollars, most people will do anything. Double-minded pastors should learn that Jesus, unlike money, is a worthy *master teacher*, because a *worthy teacher* is an example (disciple) of his own teaching. Jesus said, "If you do not believe me for what I say, then follow me, and believe me for my works." Jesus can calm even the anxiety fears of the double-minded pastors about the uncertainties of life, so that in the final analysis they will not need more, want more, or have to have more **(Matt. 6:25–34): "For this reason I say to you, do not be anxious for your life, as to what you shall eat, or what you shall drink; nor for your body, as to what you shall put on. Is not life more than food and the body more than clothing? Look at the birds of the air, they do not sow, neither do they reap, nor gather into barns, and yet their Heavenly Father feeds them. Are you not worth much more than they? And which of you by being anxious can add a single cubit to his life's span? . . . But seek first His Kingdom and His righteousness; and all these things shall be added to you. Therefore do not be anxious for tomorrow; for tomorrow will care for itself."** Each day has enough trouble of its own. The gospel writer is simply declaring that life is to be lived one day at a time since tomorrow is not

promised. *Time* belongs to God; he is *time*. Humans are granted a certain number of years between birth and death. According to the Noah and the Ark story, the lifespan of a human being is potentially 120 years. However, since the wages of sin is death, life expectancy is traditionally thought to be seventy years.

In other words, God gives individuals 120 years of physical life (*space in time*) to morally integrate flesh and spirit, to become spiritually in fellowship with God. In short, there is a dash between entrance (birth) and death (exit). What an individual does with the dash is about personal choices and responsibilities, and of course, choices have consequences.

The church must become the church beyond the church or, as some have rightly declared, the "*church without walls.*" Herein lies the crux of the problem: the church has become a middle-class corporate institution that has turned inward to serve its own *EGO* interests (edging God out) rather than the needs of the community. **"Take heed therefore unto yourselves, and to all the flock, over which the Holy Ghost hath made you overseers, to feed the Church of God, which He has purchased with His own blood" (Acts 20:28**). There is always a temptation to pervert the truth and maximize relativism. The church of God must be fed with the "principles of God," and God's principles do not change from one generation to the next (as relativism would want people to believe).

Jesus is the Good Shepherd. The undershepherd (pastor) of a local church congregation must feed the sheep, not eat the sheep. Pastors are called to rightfully stand and divide the word of truth, at all costs. For if a pastor does not tell the people "thus says the Lord your God," then the blood is on his hands. There was a great preacher by the name of Andrew Melville who was informed that King James VI of England would be present in church and that he should be careful about not offending the king. When Melville got up to preach, he said, "Melville, Melville, be mindful of what you say; the king is here today." Melville repeated the sentence several times, and then Melville said, "Melville, be careful what you say; the *King of Kings* is here every day." A pastor must love people in the same manner that Jesus loved people and the church.

Therefore, a real pastor must pastor people with *love and service*, not money. In the first century, Jesus chased the money changers out of the temple. Today, in the twenty-first century, the money changers are back and stronger than ever; because there are more of them, they recruit each other. Double-minded pastors are trying to pastor church buildings with money while leaving people spiritually unfed; their objective is to build physical monuments to themselves, but that is an abandonment of the *principles of God*. The Mount of Transfiguration story is a stark reminder of the dangers of building physical temples. Jesus desired to demonstrate to Peter, James, and John the power of God that lies within individuals and to teach them how to access that power in order that they might be able to empower others. Once they experienced the magnitude of the internal *power of God*, they in turn wanted to build three temples (churches): one to Jesus, one to Moses, and one to Elijah. Jesus declared, "I did not demonstrate this power [*the power within*] to you to start a conversation about erecting temples, but to build productive spiritual lives. God's principles do not change. Once you are fed spiritually with the principles of God, you will go into the world and save the world, for this is the mission of the church." Jesus was crucified in order that the world might be saved.

The mission of the church is to save the world: one community at a time. For God so loved the world that he gave...but if we are cowards we will never leave the premises (the *church-house building*), because we do not understand the promise. In the black community, there is a church house on every corner, and yet black-on-black crime is the most frequent form of immoral criminal activity in American society. Again, the question is, why? And again, the answer is that the church has lost its moral power to speak the truth in love and above all to speak truth to *power*. Double-minded pastors are primarily promoting preaching as an entertainment style, not as a means of telling the truth. This is vividly true in the black community. Sermons in the black church community are designed to make churchgoers feel good (emotionalize), not to help them understand redemptive salvation for their sins; since an individual cannot live free from sin, we must learn how to live free of the penalty of sin, because sin is self-infliction. *Self is the enemy*, because sin makes individuals their own enemy. The penalty of sin is spiritual death. Sermons, however, do not preach this. In short, sermons are psychological tension reduction mechanisms, or mental therapy. Therefore, church attendance becomes a psychological tension reduction mechanism rather than a medium of spiritual development for feeding the soul.

Again, the Mount of Transfiguration story—with Peter, James, and John—is powerfully applicable. The Mount of Transfiguration was about the elevation of human thoughts to a higher spiritual dimension of consciousness about the power of God that resides in each individual. Peter, James, and John thought that Jesus was showing them how to glorify themselves by building monuments (church edifices) to their leadership. Just like the disciples, double-minded pastors have power and do not know what to do with it. In other words, double-minded pastors desire to build temples and church houses for self-edification and self-glorification. On the one hand, double-minded pastors want church houses that look like they are focused on heaven but have their back doors open to the world. On the other hand, God desires churches where *love* works miracles, because wherever the spirit of God is, miracles will be performed. Today, we do not have churches that are full of *miracles*, but churches that are full of worldly mess. For after all, double-minded pastors do not have the patience of God. They want the materialistic things of this world *quick*, right *now*, and in a *hurry*. **"Those who hear the Word of God do so with an honest and good heart and bear fruit with patience" (Luke 8:15).**

Double-minded pastors are in a hurry to go nowhere. I know of one double-minded pastor (a bishop) who was riding around in a *Silver Streak Rolls Royce* in the ghetto asking to be beaten, mugged, and robbed. Jesus turned the world upside down on *foot*, not in an Oldsmobile, BMW, Cadillac, or Rolls Royce. Jesus rode on a borrowed donkey one time and in a boat one time—and of course, the one time he was in a boat he had to calm the elements (wind and waves) by declaring, "*Peace, be still.*" Indeed, in the twenty-first century the spirit of Jesus can calm the raging storms in our individual lives. A Christian must run the race with patience: All the days of my life, I will wait on the Lord.

God is patiently waiting for his children to turn from their wicked ways and return back to *him*, to *his* principles. God says that if we are patient, we will be able to walk and not become weary, run and not faint, and ultimately mount up with the wings of eagles, and as Christians we can fly in our minds above the confusion of this old world. Moreover, Jesus declared that the things that he did, greater things shall we do. We can transform our church houses into places where love works miracles by teaching and demonstrating three things:

1. How to go to church before we come to church.
2. How to repair lives in order that individuals might live creative religious lives individually and within the family context.
3. How to share the love of God that was expressed in how Jesus lived and above all why he was crucified, not how he died.

In order to liberate churchgoers, we must teach them how to go to church before they come to church (church in the home). This process is about bringing meaning to the church house, rather than coming to the church house looking for meaning. The institutional church is broken, because too many of our families are broken. Unfortunately, black churches, by and large, consist not of whole families, but of women, children, and the elderly. Therefore, we must teach and exemplify strategies for repairing spiritual brokenness in families: Preach the truth and hide behind the cross of Jesus Christ.

Once this occurs in our churches, we can effectively share the love of God that was in Jesus Christ, reconciling us to each other and us unto God. But more importantly, when this happens we will have churches where love works miracles and where individuals are able to outrun the devil (evil). Double-minded pastors then will be out of business. For God has said, "I will give you pastors after your own heart." The black community especially needs kingdom-building churches, not corporate prosperity churches that are solely oriented towards expressions of vulgar materialism, typified in many instances by the lifestyles of double-minded pastors. On the one hand, these individuals have expensive cars, jets, and helicopters, and powerful television ministries, but cannot have an effect on the moral decline of American society, especially in minority neighborhoods. On the other hand, Jesus changed the course of human history (the world) on *foot*. We have a serious "*moral order*" problem in our nation in general—especially in *minority and ethnic communities*. Minority-on-minority crime is a testament to this social fact. This brings us full circle to a profound question: What kind of *church universal* do we need?

The answer is that we need one focused on the theology of God. The theology of God is about *greatness*, because individuals were created for *greatness*. God created human beings in his own image and likeness (Genesis 1:27). The image of God is spiritual, not anthropological. Individuals were created for both spiritual as well as cultural greatness. Greatness is not about what we can get others to do for us, but what we do for ourselves in relationship to what we do for others (service). Indeed, God does not judge us on the basis of sin because he has made provision for the forgiveness of sins; the wages of sin is death, but the *gift of God* is eternal life. Therefore, God judges us on the basis of the good left undone, those *good deeds* that we could do to make life more *God centered* but which we do not choose to do because of greed, envy, and jealousy. In biblical language this is called the principle of reaping what you sow. The secular world would say, "*What goes around comes around,*" and of course, the law of gravity declares that "*what goes up must come down.*" Double-minded pastors have not embraced this theological perspective about the principles of God.

Double-minded pastoral leadership is quick and in a hurry to deliver messages regarding material prosperity, not spiritual prosperity (the *fruits of the Spirit*), by thanking God for health and soundness of mind (mental capacity). Instead, many of these pastoral leaders bleed the less fortunate with materialistic messages about tithing. Seldom, if ever, do these pastoral leaders deliver a message based upon the teachings of Jesus concerning tithing: **"Woe unto you, Scribes and Pharisees, hypocrites! For ye pay tithe of mint and anise and cumin, and have omitted the weightier matters of the law, judgment, mercy, and faith: These ought ye to have done, and not leave the other undone. Ye blind guides, which strain at a gnat, and swallow a camel. Woe unto**

you, Scribes and Pharisees, hypocrites! For ye make clean the outside of the cup and of the platter, but within they are full of extortion and excess" (Matt. 23:23–25).

Let me be perfectly clear about the contrast. The double-minded pastor is caught up in the *Old Testament* using scriptural truths concerning tithing for personal gain, rather than using the spiritual truths Jesus refers to in the New Testament as the basis for giving and spiritual enlightenment. *Real* investment, therefore, is not in materialistic things but in faith and obedience towards the will of God (*love and service*), because God has no physical needs. "Seek ye first the kingdom of God and his righteousness and all other things will be added unto you." God is the author and finisher of our *faith,* and he has promised a heavenly reward.

To be in a right relationship with God is what freedom is all about (he gives us free will). Therefore, in the religion of Jesus materialistic things are not symbols of wealth but rather are signs of lost and wasted wealth. The devil rewards with materialistic things up front because he has no reward for the back side, only damnation through spiritual torment. God rewards on the front side and throughout life as well as on the back side after love and service. Materialistic things do not make us free but rather make us *prisoners* of the *devil, because the devil has no spiritual righteousness,* and we are forced to have to work like the *devil* to pay for them or to keep them. But, on the other hand, once an individual has reached the level of spiritual independence and spiritual prosperity (*fruits of the Spirit*) that the Bible reveals as absolute truth, individuals will discover that they have less need for *materialistic junk* in their lives. Finally, God has truly blessed America. The real question of the twenty-first century is: Will American pastoral leadership now bless God through obedience to his divine will and spiritual purposes through love and service to others?

PRAYER

In times like these, we pray for the *church universal* and that love and service will always abide as the foundational tenets of who we say we are: *Christians*, being dutifully Christlike through love and service in Jesus' name. To God be the *glory*. Fix the *church*; fix the problem(s). God says, "Stop! Look! Listen! The church belongs to my only begotten Son, Jesus Christ; I can and I will fix the church." Amen.

CHAPTER EIGHT

SAVE THE CHILDREN: THE GIFT OF GOD

"God is a Spirit: and they that worship *Him* must worship *Him* in spirit and truth" (John 4:24). We are flesh and blood; we cannot serve God directly, as he is spirit, so we serve God indirectly through love, service, and sacrifice to others. No one more than our children need our love, service, and sacrifices, since they are God's gift to us. I am including a personal testimony at this point. My son, Daryl Anthony Mills, was in his freshmen year of college at the University of Houston-Central. When he received his first semester grades, he earned an A in tennis. I was extremely disappointed that he did not receive A's in all of his subjects. When I discussed the matter with him, I started to *cry,* and then he started to *cry* as well. Through his tears he said, "Dad, you love me too much." Through my tears I replied, "No, son. I'm trying to *teach* you how to love yourself, because a *parent* can never love a child too much." I was simply seeking to help my son understand that life is about *priorities* and *prioritizing*; understanding how to put things in *order* of importance. To the parents of the world, I submit that we need to love our children more than life itself, because our children are indeed a heritage from God. **"Lo, children are a heritage of the Lord: And the fruit of the womb is His reward" (Psalms 127:3).** Indeed, children are our future, and how we deal with parenting and stewardship in relationship to their futures defines the quality of our spiritual heritage (heaven on earth). These are truly difficult and troubling times in which we live. Our children are being socialized and programmed for failure, not success. **Proverbs 22:6** declares, **"Train up a child in the way he should go: When he is old, he will not depart from it."** The struggle for the minds of our children is about the popular-culture environment where they are being socialized into becoming kids—which is to say, becoming hardheaded.

It is the environment, stupid! It is the home, stupid! It is the church house, stupid! It is the schoolhouse, stupid! It is the gang mentality, stupid! It is the peer group influence, stupid! It is the society, stupid! It is me, O Lord! Children are important God-given gifts in the kingdom of God—so much so that when Jesus was confronted by his disciples with the question of who is the greatest in the kingdom of God, Jesus answered the question with an illustration. **"Whosoever shall receive this child in my name receives me; and whosoever shall receive me receives Him that sent me: For he that is least among you all, the same shall be great" (Luke 9:46–48).**

Remember the very individuals that Jesus had called out of their self-centered lifestyles to become fishers of men (*soul savers*) are now mumbling and grumbling about "who is the greatest." Jesus tells them to *be quiet.* He places a child by his side and declares that we must humble ourselves; we must have the humility of a child if we desire to be great. Then Jesus proceeds to the *upper room* and takes off his royal robe. Fills a pail with water and washes the feet of the disciples (*an act of love and service*). If we want to become great, we must be willing to serve others. If we want to be great, we should not embrace *self-promotion or bragging.* To be sure, if we want to be great, we should not forget God, and most of all individuals should not forget *God's love law:* love God and love our neighbors as ourselves; these are flip sides of the same coin. But most of all, remember: **"Blessed is the man that walks not in the counsel of the ungodly, nor stands in the way of sinners, nor sits in the seat of the scornful" (Psalms 1:1).**

Double-minded pastors are tearing down and erecting one church building after another—bigger and more elaborate and ornate church houses. Millions of dollars are being tied up ("*invested*") in buildings for self-glorification and pastoral competition, and above all very meager resources are being allocated to ministering to the needs of the nation's children. These *sleeping giants* are open for *worship* on Sundays and Wednesdays and closed for *love* and *service (benevolence)* on Mondays, Tuesdays, Thursdays, Fridays, and Saturdays. While this sad state of affairs prevails, our children are living in hell, not going to hell in a handbasket. The book of **James (1:27)** declares that **"Pure religion and undefiled before God the Father is this, to visit the fatherless and widows in their affliction, and to keep yourself unspotted before the world." "Submit yourselves therefore to God. Resist the devil, and he will flee from you" (James 4:7). "But be ye doers of the word, and not hears only, deceiving your own selves. Or if any be a hearer of the word, and not a doer, he is like unto a man beholding his natural face in a glass: For he beholdeth himself, and goeth his way, and straight-way forgetteth what manner of man he was" (James 1:22)**. The Good Shepherd (Jesus) was *the* doer of the word, and therefore his undershepherds should also be doers of the word, not just preachers of the word.

I am reminded of the rich man who got so caught up in wealth and self-glorification that he declared that he was going to tear down his barns and build bigger barns in order to hoard more goods. God sits high and looks low. Consequently, the spirit of God paid him a little visit and said *thy fool* this night your *soul* is required of thee; then who will all of this *junk* belong to **(Matt. 5:22 and Luke 12:20)**? Jesus said, **"I come that you might have life, and life more abundantly."** Since our days are numbered, the only way for us to have life more abundantly is by loving, protecting, and serving *God's precious gift* to us—our children. **"It is not meet to take the children's bread, and cast it to dogs" (Matt. 15:26)**. On the one hand, as a society we have been taking both spiritual and physical bread from our children; we have given our children over to a *flesh* worldly orientation towards life, maximizing the pleasure principle. Instead, as Christians we are duty *obligated* to be in the world, but not of the world. Therefore, the best spiritual investment as Christians that we can make is indeed in our children and their future, because without children we really eternally die. If no one is having children or nurturing them, we are already dead (eternal bone-fire). When men do not provide material substance and spiritual/moral protection for their children, they in fact have already lost their souls to the "devil" in this world before they physically die.

Therefore, since one is sterile and the other is deadly for children, same-sex marriage and abortion are not a part of *God's divine salvation plan* for humanity; they are issues that the church should never, ever embrace as they do not fit into God's spiritual plan of soul salvation: Be fruitful, multiply, replenish and subdue the earth. **"Who will rise up for me against the evildoers? Or who will stand up for me against the workers of iniquity?" (Psalms 94:16)**. Of course, this is not the first time this question has been asked. The question is: Who will say, **"Here I am, Lord, send me!" (Isaiah 6:8)**. Jeremiah in his anguish cried out, **"O that my head were waters, and mine eyes a fountain of tears, that I might weep day and night for the slain of the daughter of my people!" (Jeremiah 9:1–9)**. Jeremiah is talking about individuals living in spiritual darkness and walking in confusion. To be sure, God and the devil (destroyer) have different plans for our individual as well as collective lives. God desires that we live by his Spirit in order that we might live eternally. The devil wants us to live by the flesh in order that we perish (die) eternally. The Christian church preaching the truth of God is the only hope for this confused world.

The Problem

When children are born into this world, the hearts of their minds are pure, even though we are born in sin and shaped in iniquity. Unfortunately, most of our children are conceived out of unbridled lust in the flesh (Galatians 5:16–19), not godly love (agape). Herein is the crux of our family and societal problem. A child *ought* to represent the *love obligation* between a man and a woman. Hence, the child should be an expression of love and consequently a *divine obligation* to the child. Today we have fathers and mothers biologically conceiving children, and not daddies and mommies spiritually responsible for teaching and training children; therefore non-sanctification exists in the home (1 Cor. 7:14). Too many *unsanctified* and *unbelieving* (*non-God-fearing*) individuals are birthing children into this world out of *lustful love confusion*; children, then, are left to be nurtured by the forces of secular cultural values, rather than family spiritual values.

We have far too many *illegitimate* adult parents birthing children into this world out of lustful sexual pleasure rather than out of godly love obligation towards each other. We also have *confused* children birthing children out of pleasure-seeking fantasies, confusing love and sexuality. Consequently, we have illegitimate parents, not illegitimate children, simply because if a child is conceived and born into this world, that child is legitimate. The concept of illegitimacy is about property rights, so if children are not born within a marriage, the children have no right to their biological father's property. Without a doubt, the child was conceived and born into the world the same way everyone else was, regardless of the status of the parental relationship.

To be sure, family is not an economic institution but a *love* association, because *divine love* created the institution of family. Families have economic functions but are not economic corporations as *some misguided public figures* would have the American people believe. *Sexual immorality* has become the *corporate business of sin*. Without a doubt, the business of sin is perpetuated by individuals who have evil minds, because the devil (destroyer) is an "*evil mind (spirit).*" God says that he is ***"angry with the wicked everyday"*** **(Psalms 7:11)**. Individuals taking right and making it wrong, and taking wrong and making it right or making it seem to work, is just about as evil as can be. God says that he will forgive us for any sin except sinning against the Holy Spirit (blasphemy), which is deliberately teaching and turning others against the truth (Mark 3:29). However, **"There is a way which seems right unto a man, but the end thereof are the ways of death" (Proverbs 14:12)**. The effect of all of this confusion is compounded in our children. Consequently, we are breeding a mindset in our children that is unclean and nonspiritual.

We know this is factual because our children invariably ask the worldly "*Janet Jackson*" question: What have you done for me lately? To be sure, we must teach our children that you cannot run nor hide from the *will of God: For* ***"it is appointed unto men once to die, but after this the judgment"*** **(Hebrews 9:27)**. As Christians we are allowing the secular world to breed a professional criminal culture of *barbarism* among our children. Parents must, therefore, in their everyday lives set the example of seeking **"first the Kingdom of God, and His righteousness; and all these things shall be added unto you" (Matt. 6:33)**. Of course, all of these things are mentioned in **Matt. 6:31: "Take no thought, what shall we eat? Or, what shall we drink? Or, wherewithal shall we be clothed?"** As families we all need to "seek ye first the Kingdom of God, and His righteousness; and all of these things shall be added unto you." Then we will be born again of the spirit of God through *faith* in his *Son* Jesus Christ (John 3:7).

God has family on his mind, and so should we as Christians. Most of all, the church should have family on its mind, not corporate money-making activities. The crux of most of our societal ills is grounded in the breakdown of family life and is a parenting problem, which in turn is grounded in the pleasure-seeking principle. Individuals cannot seek to have a good time all the time. The only place whereby the sun shines mostly all the time is in the desert, and of course, things burn up in the desert. Therefore, in every life rain must fall, because there is purpose in pain. No pain, no gain. Sexuality is God's gift to us when it is exercised in the context of godly love.

In the scientific world, *TNT* equals dynamite. In the spiritual world, *TNT* is "teaching and training": mothers teaching children about love (respect towards self and others), and fathers training (instilling self-discipline in) children in the *way of the Lord*. A father must rule over his home with love, not money. King Solomon declared that only a fool in his heart (mind) will say that money solves all things.

Family life is about love and respect, not material goodies. Giving children things instead of parental love is not a good parenting strategy. God did not create *mess* or confusion. **"For God is not the author of confusion, but of peace, as in all churches of the saints" (1 Cor. 14:33).** God created peace and harmony in the universe. God created an orderly real world, because God has a logical mind, not an illogical mind. **"Let this mind be in you, which was also in Christ Jesus" (Philippians 2:5).** God wants us to think with the logic of our minds, not our emotions. Again, scripture says. let the mind that was in Christ Jesus be also in you.

The devil is a spirit, similar to how God is a spirit, but the devil wants you to think with your emotions. Of course, if you think with your emotions you will always deal with the flesh (external world) rather than the Spirit. Seemingly what is going on with our children is they are being taught by the world to think with the flesh and therefore seek instant gratification, the end result being: **"There is a way that seems right unto a man, but the end thereof are the ways of death" (Proverbs 14:12).** Families in conjunction with churches should be working in tandem with the Beatitudes to provide a spiritual vision for America's children in Jesus' name.

The Bible says, **"My people are destroyed for lack of knowledge: Because thou have rejected knowledge, I will also reject thee, that thou shalt be no priest to me: Seeing thou hast forgotten the law of thy God, I will also forget thy children" (Hosea 4:6).** It is a commonly held thought that preachers' children tend to be the most misbehaved and undisciplined children in the church. I wonder why? Could the above scripture have the answer to the *why* question? Without a doubt, the breakdown of the family unit is at the center of all of the confusion that is being heaped upon the heads of our children. The one place where *all of us* should meet God in partnership is in the *family context*, and therefore, because this is not occurring, we are lost to God and alive to greed, strife, jealousy, selfishness, and above all *idolatry*.

Jesus lifted up the concept of humanity (humankind), and we have a new image to live up to. We cannot teach character like we teach math. Character must be caught or inspired by *example*. Indeed, a worthy teacher is always an example of his or her own teaching. Jesus said, "If you do not believe me for what I say, then believe me for my works' sake." It is not a question of knowing what is right, but of having the moral courage to do what is right. Moral failure need not be a disgrace if an individual faces it with honesty and without illusions. **"He hath shown thee, O man, what is good; and what doth the Lord require of thee, but to do justly, and to love mercy, and to walk humbly with thy God?" (Micah 6:8). Isaiah 54:13** declares, **"All thy children shall be taught by the Lord; and great shall be the peace of thy children."** Too many fathers are absent from the family life of their children and thereby are provoking their children to wrath. **Ephesians 6:4** says, **"And, ye fathers, provoke not your children to wrath, but bring them up in the nurture and admonition of the Lord."** Our children are victimized by absentee fathers, vanity-oriented mothers, and most of all a philosophy of me, myself and I, where flesh is oriented towards secularism.

Without a doubt, the breakdown of the family as a *spiritual unit* based upon love is the defining cause of *all* our societal ills. As a result, we have misguided men and guided missiles. The problem is that too many churches have turned inward, serving their own institutional needs, and too few churches are lovingly serving humanity. *Charity* (love) begins at home and then spreads abroad. Even many so-called foreign mission operations are designed primarily for personal gain: charity begins at home; we do not have to go looking for problems to solve in foreign lands. This statement is not intended as some kind of rejection of foreign missions, but we should clean up our own front yard before we attempt to clean up someone else's backyard. **"Go ye into the world, and preach the gospel to every creature" (John 16:15)**. Again, the church must love and serve as God has commanded. Jesus only sent the disciples out to serve others after they had been prepared to minister to others. **"But grow in grace, and in the knowledge of our Lord and Savior Jesus Christ. To him be glory both now and forever" (2 Peter 3:18).**

In fact, because marriage is viewed almost exclusively as a civil contract overseen by civil courts rather than a spiritual union overseen by the church as a sacred sacrament, the concept of civil pre-nuptials was *legally* instituted. So *when* we break up, this is the amount of *money* to which each of us is entitled. In this framework marriage is about *property rights*, not about a spiritual union under the authority of God. Consequently, our children are not being nurtured in spiritual environments, but rather environments that are overwhelmingly materialistic and money driven. Families must get back to tough love/disciplinary love based upon a moral foundation of godly spiritual righteousness and moral character traits, rather than *lustful* pleasure oriented towards materialism. Simply put, adults must act like adults. Parents must learn how to be parents and not seek to be our child's friend. When we are good parents, we are our child's best friend. Unfortunately, far too many children are growing up with an entitlement mentality that someone owes them something. They need to learn an important life lesson. Someone does owe them, and of course they are that someone, and they can pay themselves through self-sacrifice and self-discipline.

From 1994 to 2003, there was a dramatic increase in gang-related activity. The *gang* became the surrogate family unit (parenting socialization unit), in conjunction with television and video technology (electronics). The gang phenomenon is primarily about physical protection rather than family nurturing. The end result is that many children do not experience *nature* but only experience a gang mentality, which is oriented towards violence and man-made electronics. An important part of experiencing God is experiencing nature, because God is in everything (omnipresence) and touched by nothing. If an individual's heart (mind) is pure, he or she can soar to heavenly places. Moses experienced this at Mount Sinai.

At this point, I want to share some startling statistical data on the wrath that is being provoked in our children by *absentee* fathers and *vanity*-oriented mothers, because the search for spiritual understanding is neither easy nor popular. Homelessness among youth is at an epidemic level in our society. For example, there are over two million homeless youth in America, with a 25 percent increase in student homelessness. One in three homeless youth are under eighteen years old. One in three homeless runaways is between the ages of fifteen and seventeen. One-third are forced to perform *deviant* sexual acts. Over one-half of the runaways have parental problems. One in three homeless youth runaways attempt suicide at some point in time. Homeless runaways are ten times more likely to be HIV positive. Ten percent of the homeless females are pregnant. Forty to fifty percent of the homeless youth have had contact with the foster-care system. (Source: Homelessness National Alliance.)

The Office of Juvenile Justice and Delinquency Prevention (OJJDP) complies arrest information provided by law enforcement agencies each year and creates reports examining the trends, rates, and statistics of juvenile criminal activity. Every four years, OJJDP publishes a comprehensive study as part of its Juvenile Offenders and Victims National Report Series. Of course, a number of crimes committed by juvenile offenders go unreported. One in 20 children have witnessed someone being shot. One in 200 children between the ages of fourteen and seventeen have witnessed a murder. One in 50 children between the ages of fourteen and seventeen have been sexually assaulted. One in 10 children between the ages of fourteen to seventeen was exposed to five or more violent crimes in 2009. At this point, we do not know the effect of violence on the long-term health and well-being of children. We can only speculate.

While juvenile crimes since 1997 are on the decline by at least 5 percent, large numbers of juvenile crimes go unreported. Roughly half of all youth arrests are made on account of theft, simple assault, drug abuse, disorderly conduct, and curfew violations. The Office of Juvenile Justice and Delinquency Prevention statistics show theft as the greatest cause of youth arrests.

There are a number of highly effective organizations across the country committed to meeting the needs of homeless abused children. One such organization is Beulah's Place. Beulah's Place began as a vision to feed hungry, homeless teens on a daily basis in order to take them out of harm's way from sexual predators, pedophiles, and deviant sexual criminal influences. These at-risk teens find unconditional love, hope, safety, and options for getting back on track for success in their young lives.

Beulah's Place is a privately funded non-profit organization with its national office and flagship shelter located in central Oregon. Plans to expand to forty states are in the works. Beulah's Place founder, Andi Buerger, is a sought after, inspirational speaker and advocate who travels internationally to create awareness for the cause of those who cannot fight for themselves. To support the fight against child trafficking and abuse through Beulah's Place, contact:

Beulah's Place
P. O. Box 518
Redmond, Oregon 97756
(541) 788–9639
www.beulahsplace.org
info@beulahsplace.org

Too many children are growing up not playing outside but playing with objects (electronics), and therefore not experiencing the reality of God. Our children cannot continue to live in this manner; therefore, we must make our streets, parks, neighborhoods, and schools, as well as all of our social institutions, safe for the sake of our children's spiritual well-being. We must come to common higher ground on one accord, the *Word of God, because the Word works.* Guns and more guns are not the answer, neither are laws such as "*stand your ground.*" Partisan politics cannot solve our nation's ills; they can only divide the *nation* that God has *allowed* to exist for over two hundred years as the basis for universal world citizenship (the earth is the *Lord's* and the fullness thereof and all that dwell therein—Psalms 24:1 and Exodus 9:29). America is the greatest nation on the planet, and of course it is not "love it or leave it," but change it or lose it. For we all know that ***"God is angry with the wicked everyday"*** **(Psalms 7:11).** Partisan politics is only a symptom of the problem, not the problem. Sadly, there is only one party with two different factions (Democratic/ Republican)—the *corporate business party*. President Eisenhower called it the *military-industrial complex.*

Church begins in the home; school also begins in the home. Children must be taught proper manners, listening and cognitive skills, and above all must be taught to ask for *permission to do all things* before entering school. **"Let all things be done decently and in order" (1 Corinthians 14:40).**

The breakdown of family life is central to an understanding of what is at the crux of the issues associated with many of our societal ills, especially the social ills that most affect the well-being of our children. In many instances, the primary focus on money in churches contributes significantly to the breakdown of family life. Therefore, because of the breakdown of family life, *sustainable values* are not being taught and exemplified in the context of family life or church life. Fathers and mothers have distinct roles that must be played out in every family context. I am not talking about *role fixation.* Indeed, fathers need to know how to cook, wash dishes and clothes, clean house, and so on. I am referencing the *spiritual roles* that women and men must understand as fathers and mothers. All children know their mother, but wise children know their father. God-given *emotional/spiritual* bonding takes place between a mother and a child at conception. For nine months, a mother emotionally and spiritually bonds with a child while the child is developing in his or her *Garden of Eden (the mother's womb), whereby life is a free gift.* The father is sitting on the sidelines watching and waiting for the birth occasion. When the child is born, the mother must now emotionally bring the father into the picture. She tells the father, "This is your child," then she tells the child, "This is your father." The father has to have *faith* that the mother is telling the *truth*. Here's where trouble (*doubt*) begins, simply because in many instances the child was conceived out of lustful *sexual love,* not godly *agape* love.

Therefore, when the mother tells the father, "This is your child," the confusion *(hell)* begins because of the lack of *godly love (agape)* based upon *faith* in God and *faith* in each other. Instead of the child being viewed as *God's gift* and received by *faith*, the child becomes mama's baby and papa's maybe. Now here comes *mass societal* confusion being played out on national television: the Maury show, the Jerry Springer Show, and above all *DNA* testing—in short, universal societal confusion. The confusion comes about because of the obligation that must now be shouldered in relationship to *provision* and *protection* for the child. The sexual fun and gamesmanship is over. No pain, no gain now comes into play. Because of these circumstances, far too many women are failing to teach children to love their fathers in order that fathers might train their children in the way of the Lord. Even if the father is absent, the mother should not teach the child to love her and hate the father, because this only heaps confusion on top of confusion. Eventually because of this confusion the children will tell their mothers, "I will do what I want to do; you are not my mother; I am grown," and they end up hating their mothers.

This type of *attitude* on the part of male children only places a brick on the next prison wall. As a consequence, far too many women are teaching their male children to love them, and the consequence is a feminized male culture—not *homosexuality*; there is a difference between the two concepts. Feminized men think with their emotions rather than the logic of their minds, and of course, this is the ideal, not the real. To be sure, you cannot train children in the way of the Lord if you think with your emotions. Confusion related to family breakdown does not lend itself to the teaching of *sustainable* values, but rather *situational* values. Women set examples and precepts. Men have visions, and unfortunately too many men are absent from their families. As a result, many families are perishing because of lack of family vision. Therefore, the family cannot function as a bridge over troubled waters. High spiritual expectations are not being set for our children in the home nor the church. In other words, our children are not being spiritualized either at home or in the church, but rather are being brutalized at home and at the church house. For example, not too long ago I was in an elementary school setting. A male second grader followed another male classmate to the restroom. While one of them was using the toilet, the second placed his private anatomy in the other's mouth. When the mother arrived at the school, she explained that her son was in psychological therapy because he had been sexually molested at church.

I am reminded of a story in the book of Acts (20:7–12) when the New Testament writer Paul was preaching to the disciples in the city of Troas. There was a young man sitting in the window, and the *church* was not paying the young man any attention and was totally involved in the religious service. The young man was in the window (*a dangerous place* in the first place), while the church was caught up in the religious services and before the children went to sleep. Paul had preached so long that the young man fell into a deep sleep, falling three stories to the ground. Everyone thought that the child was dead. Paul went down and fell on the child, embracing him, and said, "He is alive." The moral of the story is this: While the church was involved in a religious service, the young man was in imminent danger, awaiting an accident to occur, but for God's intervention.

In modern America, our children are in imminent danger, waiting not only for accidents to occur, but creating incidents of sin and iniquity to participate in. Families cannot become families until churches become the church. My prayer for the children of America comes directly from the Bible as well as professional public school and college/university teaching experiences.

Know that **"He that dwelleth in the secret place of the most high shall abide under the shadow of the Almighty. He shall call upon me, and I shall answer him, I will be with him in trouble; I will deliver him, and honor him. With long life will I satisfy him and shew him my salvation" (Psalms 91:1–15–16)**. The faithful know that **"the fear of the Lord prolongeth days: But the years of the wicked shall be shortened" (Proverbs 10:27). "Seeing ye have purified your souls in obeying the truth through the spirit unto unfeigned love of the brethren, see that ye love one another with a pure heart fervently" (1 Peter 1:27)**. All Christians should know that in the end, **"Though I have the gift of prophecy, and understand all mysteries, and all knowledge, and though I have all faith, so that I could remove mountains, and have not charity, I am nothing. Charity suffereth long, and is kind, charity envieth not; charity vaunteth not itself, is not puffed up, doth not behave itself unseemly, seeketh not her own, is not easily provoked, thinketh no evil; Rejoiceth not in iniquity, but rejoiceth in the truth; beareth all things, endureth all things. Charity never faileth: But whether there be prophecies, they shall fail; whether there be tongues, they shall cease . . . And now abideth faith, hope, charity, but the greatest of these is charity"**

(1 Corinthians 13:2–13). In this book I have given God my very best, and of course my prayer is: *Share the love.*

The truth is, families cannot *reorient* themselves towards love and self-sacrifice while churches *appear* to be caught up in materialism and self-serving institutional ego gratification. So goes the church universal, so goes the world. So goes the family, so goes the world. So goes the family, so goes the church, because when you have broken families, you have broken churches. It goes without saying that when the church is not at the center of community life, the community suffers. Therefore, the Christian church is in need of a *second reformation.* Because of the sin of *one* man (Adam) we needed a second Adam (Jesus Christ), who was sinless. Now because of the sin(s) of *many* churches we need a *second reformation* in order to reestablish the *church of Jesus Christ.* A reformation not based upon the Ninety-Five Theses of Martin Luther, but the *Two Great Commandments* of the King of Kings: Jesus Christ.

Jesus Is the Answer: Jesus Is the Light of the World

As a society, we are in a bad situation. We have created a spiritual prison for our children as well as for ourselves (society). Churches need to institute classes on being spiritual mothers and spiritual fathers as the only way out of this horrible mess in which we find ourselves.

This is the church's alternative to the *Caesar way*, which is prison after prison and more prisons. American society has its own twenty-first century Egypt; America's back is indeed against the wall. **Psalm 82:1–5** declares that **"God stands in the congregation of the *mighty*; He judges among the gods. How long will ye judge unjustly, and accept the persons of the wicked? Selah. Defend the poor and the fatherless: Do justice to the afflicted and needy. Deliver the poor and needy; rid them out of the hand of the wicked. They know not, neither will they understand; they walk on in darkness: All the foundations of the earth are out of course."**

Jesus spoke in parables, and oftentimes individuals did not understand his message. On one such occasion, Jesus in the gospel of **John (10:7–16)** declares, **"Verily, verily, I say unto you, I am the door of the sheep. All that ever came before me are thieves and robbers: But the sheep did not hear them. I am the door: By me if any man enters in, he shall be saved, and shall go in and out, and find pasture. The thief cometh not, but for to steal, and kill, and to destroy; I am come that they might have life, and that they might have it more abundantly. I am the good shepherd: The good shepherd gives his life for the sheep. But he that is a hireling, and not the good shepherd, whose own the sheep are not, sees the wolf coming, and leaves the sheep, and flees: And the wolf catches them, and scatters the sheep. The hireling flees, because he is a hireling, and cares not for the sheep. I am the good shepherd, and know my sheep and am known of mine. As the Father knows me, even so know I the Father: And I lay down my life for the sheep. And other sheep I have, which are not of this fold; them also I must bring, and they shall hear my voice; and there shall be one fold, and one shepherd."**

God says that *his word* is to be used for saving souls, to keep *his* children out of the fire *(physical/spiritual hell).*

Double-minded pastors are putting God's children in the fire for personal gain. God said to the church in Pergamos, **"I have a two-edged sword" (Revelation 2:13–1): "I know thy works and where thou dwells, even where Satan's seat is: And thou holds fast to my name, and hast not denied my faith, even in those days wherein Antipas was my faithful martyr, who was slain among you, where Satan dwells. But I have a few things against thee, because thou hast there them that hold the doctrine of Balaam, who taught Balak to cast a stumbling block before the children of Israel, to eat things sacrificed unto idols, and to commit fornication." Jesus said, "Do not think that I have come to bring peace on the earth; I did not come to bring peace, but a sword."** We are in a spiritual war: love versus hate and truth versus a lie. Those who say "Peace, peace," where there is no moral order do not understand peace. On the one hand, in the world community the basis for moral order is militarism. On the other hand, the basis for moral order in the family as well as the church must be God-centered morality.

A tremendous part of the answer to resolving our societal ills is that pastors must resist seeking *self-glorification*, but must rather embrace sanctification and rectification, and above all seek justification by God. **Romans 12:3** says, **"For I say, through the grace given to me, to every man among you, not to think himself more highly than he ought to think; but to think soberly, according as God has dealt to every man a measure of faith." "God is not the author of confusion, but of peace, as in all**

churches of the saints" (1 Cor. 13:33). We have moral chaos, and this moral chaos is reflected in the fact that both parents as well as the churches have failed our children—generation after generation. **"But let all things be done decently and in order" (1 Cor. 14:40). "For now we see through a glass, darkly, but then face to face, now I know in part, but then shall I know even also as I am known" (1 Cor. 13:12). "Be not deceived: Evil communications corrupt good manners" (1 Cor. 15:33). "Be not deceived; God is not mocked: For whatsoever a man sow, that shall he also reap" (Gal. 6:7). James 1:22–24** says, **"Prove yourself as doers of the Word and not merely hearers, who delude themselves. For if anyone is a hearer of the Word and not a doer, he is like a man who looks at his natural face in the mirror and immediately forgets what kind of person he is." "Submit yourselves therefore to God. Resist the devil, and he will flee from you" (James 4:7). Galatians 6:2–8** says, **"Bear one another's burdens and thus fulfill the Law of Christ. For if anyone thinks he is something when he is nothing, he deceives himself. But let each one examine his own work, and then he will have reason for boasting in himself alone, and not in regard to another. Do not be deceived, God is not mocked, for whatsoever a man sows this he will also reap. For if you sow to your own flesh, you shall reap corruption, if you sow to the Spirit you shall reap eternal life."**

All of us need to seek God's permission to use *his* body in which *his* Holy Spirit is housed. **"Know ye not that your body is the Temple of the Holy Ghost which is in you, which ye have of God, and ye are not your own? For ye are bought with a price;**

therefore glorify God in your body, and in your spirit, which are God's" (1 Cor. 6:19–20). The Psalmist declares, **"Some trust in chariots, and some trust in horses: But we will remember the name of the Lord, our God" (Psalm 20:7)**. When God punished Cain for killing his brother rather than being his brother's keeper, Cain declared that his punishment was too great. Cain's declaration ought to be a forewarning to double-minded pastoral leaders. In **Jude 1:1**, God says, **"Woe unto them! For they have gone the way of Cain, and ran greedily after the error of Balaam for reward, and perished in the gainsaying of Core."**

Blind chance does not govern life. Life is a response to our deepest yearnings and highest aspirations. God is *love,* and God says that life is a sharing of responsibility—that is, the infinite obligation that each individual owes to other human beings to love and serve. The only way that we as humans can attain this level of consciousness about the meaning of life is to understand that the soul does not record time, only growth toward love and service. **"For all have sinned, and come short of the glory of God" (Romans 3:23)**. However, I am compelled to say, all but *one:* Jesus, Jesus, Jesus.

Jesus was said to be a great *teacher* sent from God, not a great *whooper* (entertainer). It is more desirable to see a great sermon lived as an example, because example is the best teacher, and of course, a worthy teacher is always an example of his or her own teaching. Jesus declared, "If you do not believe me for what I say, then believe me for my works' sake." Finally, **"Keep yourselves in the love of God, looking for the mercy of our Lord Jesus Christ unto eternal life. And of some have compassion,**

making a difference; and others save with fear, pulling them out of the fire; hating even the garment spotted by flesh. Now unto Him that is able to keep you from falling, and to present you faultless before the presence of His glory with exceeding joy, to the only wise God our savior, be glory and majesty, dominion and power, both now and ever. Amen" (Jude 1:21–25). Fix the *church*; fix the problem(s). Amen: so be it.

EPILOGUE

THE EARTH IS THE LORD'S

How great God is. **"For He hath made Him to be sin for us, who knew no sin; that we might be made the righteousness of God in Him" (2 Corinthians 5:21).** To God be the glory! How great are we *missing* the *leadership mark!* **"Nevertheless the foundation of God standeth sure, having this seal; The Lord knoweth them that are His. And, let everyone that nameth the name of Christ depart from iniquity" (2 Timothy 2:19).** God is still angry over wickedness every day, even though he casts our *sins* into the lake of *forgetfulness* (except for *blasphemy).* Sin is self-infliction; therefore, God forgives us for becoming our own enemy (self is the enemy), since *he* is our eternal friend. But God will not forgive us for trying to make *him* our enemy (blasphemy) rather than allowing him to be our friend, which, in turn, is seeking to make God a liar. In other words, this is making *mockery* of God, trying to make it seem as though God does not know what he is doing. God hates lies, since lying is the beginning of sin. Therefore, **"who His own self bare our sins in His own body on the tree, that we, being dead to sins, should live unto righteousness: By whose stripes ye were healed" (1 Peter 2:24)**. The gospel of Matthew states, **"For this is my blood of the New Testament, which is shed for many for the remission of sins" (Matt. 26:28)**.

There is a popularized song that declares that God has the whole world in his hands. He's got the little bitty baby in his hands. He's got you and me, brother, in his hands. He's got you and me, sister, in his hands. He's got everybody in his hands. He's got the whole world in his hands. Indeed, **"The earth is the Lord's, and the fullness thereof; the world, and they that dwell therein. For he hath founded it upon the seas, and established it upon the floods. Who shall ascend into the hills of the Lord? Or who shall stand in His holy place? He that hath clean hands, and a pure heart; who hath not lifted up His soul unto vanity, nor sworn deceitfully. He shall receive the blessing from the Lord and righteousness from the God of His salvation" (Psalms 24:1–5)**.

To be sure, my *Christian friends,* anytime a *(Jewish) Christian* religion/church centers itself upon a human personality, it is not of God but is rather a personality/money cult. A Christian religion must be centered upon God and *his* spiritual values. Above all, a Christian religion is Christlike, based upon the teachings of Jesus Christ as he reiterated the Great Commandments. **"The first of all the commandments is, Hear, O Israel; the Lord our God is one Lord: And thou shall love the Lord thy God with all thy**

heart: And with all thy soul, and with all thy mind, and with all thy strength: This is the first commandment. And the second is like it, namely this, Thou shalt love thy neighbor as thyself. There is none other commandment greater than these" (Mark 12:29–31). God is God; there is no other, and there is nothing impossible for God. Without a doubt, God holds our breath in his hands as well as the breath of double-minded pastors.

Therefore, this book is not written to confuse nor disillusion *Christian believers* concerning the teachings, concepts, and precepts of our Lord and Savior Jesus Christ, because that would be blasphemy, and of course blasphemy is the unforgiveable sin. But, rather, the objective is to expose the disturbing immoral facts concerning the *teachings* as well as *actions* of double-minded pastors concerning material prosperity: by twisting God's holy Word and taking his holy name in vain for material gains. Obviously, some double-minded pastors feel that they do not have to be accountable to God nor church members. Thankfully, there are some Christians that are accountable. There is great value in Christians learning to share ideas and experiences with each other, because there is *wisdom* in sharing. Indeed, it is easy for our thinking to go astray when we grapple with the wilds of the world in isolation. All of us must learn how to take on the challenges of integrating biblical truths with our own personal lifestyles, in our home life, in school, at work, and in society in general.

Christians oftentimes say that *"God is so good all the time, and all the time God is good."* To be sure, the moral crisis facing America has become a new way for God to show his divine authority over life and creative problem-solving abilities, because humankind's extremity is God's opportunity to do anything but fail. Paul and Silas prayed, and their prayers and their praise produced a jailhouse rock unparalleled in human history; not even Elvis's "Jailhouse Rock" can touch the one produced by God, because once God unlocks the jailhouse cells, individuals ask, "What must I do to be saved?" And the answer is: **"Believe in the Lord Jesus, and you shall be saved, you and your household" (Acts 16:22–31).**

PRAYER

Merciful God, make us mindful that it is not how long we live that counts, but how we live that truly matters. For we are mindful of the fact that Methuselah lived 963 years, and the Bible only records that he lived and died, but made no contribution. However, when God called him home, he said, "Is my time up?" We know through your precepts and concepts what is required of us, God the Father: To be justly, to love mercy, and to walk humbly with God (Micah 6:8). Help us, God, so to live in order that we might confess in thy Word and walk in thy Word, in order that others might not only hear good words, but see good deeds. In Jesus' name we pray these things, and to God be the glory. Fix the church; fix the problem(s). God says, "Stop! Look! Listen! The church belongs to my only begotten Son, Jesus Christ; I can and I will fix the church." Amen!

ACKNOWLEDGMENTS

Grateful appreciation is extended to Clara M. Bowman for assistance with the processing of the manuscript; Amy Graeser for help with editing; Carolyn A. Crump for book cover artwork design; and Minister Paul W. Smith and Dr. James J. Cunningham for assistance with proofreading the manuscript. A debt of spiritual gratitude is also extended to Minister Lewis C. Parker, Jr., for our ministerial friendship over the years. Profound appreciation is extended to my dear police administrator friends Chief James A. Young and Lt. Bruce D. Jackson for assistance with the juvenile crime statistics included in chapter 8, "Save the Children." Finally, a special expression of heartfelt gratitude is extended to Charles W. Moore for our many profound and enlightening philosophical discussions over the years concerning the socio-religious nature of the human condition.

ABOUT THE AUTHOR

Bobby Eugene Mills is a *Born Again Christian; God-fearing-man*. He is an accomplished college professor and public sector administrator. Bobby earned a B.D. in theology from Colgate Rochester Divinity School and a PhD in sociology from Syracuse University. He has written and published numerous articles concerning the pressing social ills confronting American society.

Printed in the USA
CPSIA information can be obtained
at www.ICGtesting.com
JSHW082343140824
68134JS00020B/1848